Prosetry Too
Artistic Heart Expression
Geoffrey K. Leigh and Marianne Lyon

Copyright © 2024 by Geoffrey K. Leigh and Marianne Lyon

All rights reserved.

No part of this publication may be reproduced, distributed, or transmitted in any form or by any means, including photocopying, recording, other electronic or mechanical methods, or by any information storage and retrieval system without the prior written permission of the author, except as permitted by U.S. copyright law. For permission requests, contact the author.

First printing, March, 2025

Library of Congress Control Number: 2025905077

ISBN: 978-0-9985966-8-6

Book cover design: Geoffrey K. Leigh using Book Brush

Formatting: Geoffrey K. Leigh using Atticus

All rights reserved. First printing in the United States of America

We dedicate Prosetry Too to our family and friends. We love you deeply
with all our hearts. Thank you for encouraging us
to continue writing and sharing our creations.

Geoffrey: To my parents, Joan and Henry Leigh, thank you
for your encouragement in writing,
for modeling creativity and problem solving.
Also to my four children, their chosen partners,
and their offspring, I appreciate your support of my writing
and your desire to hear and share stories.

Marianne: To my husband, Jim Lyon, you have been a listener
and a supporter of all my writing endeavors.
Your partnership, steadfastness, and love sustain me.

To our poet and writer friends, we thank you so much for nudging us
to follow our dreams and create this book,
to inspire others to write their own fruitful creations.

To our dear friends and colleagues who contributed to this volume,
deep gratitude and thanks. Your support and gifted writing
enhances what we have purveyed.

To our readers, we encourage you to keep reading and writing,
in whatever form stimulates the creative side of you.
And take the risk to keep sharing your work wherever possible,
hearing viable suggestions and making the final decisions.

Contents

Introduction	1
1. 1st Episode Playing with Poetry	5
2. 2nd Episode Juxtapose Form and Feeling	23
3. 3rd Episode Prosetry	61
4. 4th Episode Short Stories and Found Prosetry	87
5. 5th Episode Resilience in Times of Terror	169
6. 6th Episode Ekphrastic Poetry and Prosetry	193
7. 7th Episode Prosetic Art	215
8. 8th Episode Prosetry from Music	233
9. About the Authors	255

Introduction

In this volumn, we use poetry, prose, and prosetry to explore the value of different formats as an expression of emotions, ideas, connections, and, in some cases, moving outside traditional boundaries in the process.

Poetry has a long history, dating back to ancient Mesopotamia and Egypt, around the 3rd Mellenium B.C.E. The oldest surviving poem, the *Epic of Gilgamesh*, written on clay tablets, told the story of a mighty king who tried to become immortal. Oral poetry, songs, or hymns may predate written texts and provide a means to share stories, history, geneology, theatrics, and social principles. Ancient poems emerged in societies around the world, from Greece, Africa, Persia, India, and China. The form spread in medieval Europe often by troubadours and later became better know by Shakespeare's many works. Modern poetry, from late 19th Centruy through the 21st, began to break with traditional forms by exploring alternative structure, language, and themes.

Below is a poem written by Marianne in our first book:

> Don't know if my aging soul has many more years
> Sages say the soul is eternal
> But I want to believe that
> my soul holds lines of verses
> a few more scribbled poems
> a folder of chiseled memoirs
> short story lessons gleaned along the way
> I'm fine with aging
> I'm fine with my wrinkles
> inside and out. (*Prosetry Journey*, p. 197)

The development of prose also traces its roots to ancient societies, particularly with the use of rhetoric in Greece. There, it flourished as an art form alongside poetry. With the spread of Latin into Europe, the orations and writings of Cicero impacted the development of prose in the medivial period. As written Arabic developed during this period, poetry and prose also became a foundation for sharing cultural and religious ideas or stories, some dating back to ancient Egypt. During the Renaissance, prose diversified by including more cultural and religious elements. During the 18th Century, the modern novel emerged and became more widespread as writing shifted to languages spoken by the common people in a country, creating wider accessibility to all forms of literature, especially with the invention of the printing press. Within fiction, compostion also includes micro fiction, short stories, novellas, and novels.

The following two paragraphs begin *The Garden*, a short story also found in our first book:

I walk out to appraise my herb garden with a mug of steaming coffee. The vessel provides toasty comfort through my hands. Rows of shoots burst out, reach for sunshine with undisguised determination to flourish, nutrified from last year's mulch and winter rains.

I notice my impatience for their maturation, anxious to explore novel health remedies. I take a deep breath, invite my body to soften, and feel into the earth as I amble along on this first short-sleeve day of spring. (p. 34).

In *Prosetry Journey* and this volumn, we explore a combination of poetry and prose we named prosetry.

By **Prosetry**, we mean some combination of prose and poetry in such a way as to make more equal contributors to the expression we are seeking. In our first book, *Prosetry Journey*, we outlined the concept and provided a few examples. But we also were still early in our own venture. The more we wrote after that book, comfort set in with both style and composition.

Below is an example of early posetry Geoffrey wrote in our first book:

INTRODUCTION

Connection Where?*

Today we consider love and connection
The attraction, passion, life's oxytocin. A flower's gentle petals, the pulling at heart strings, songs caressing a meter beat
Two beings, alive, ecstasy.

What if such seeking is distraction, or even projection of self on other?
Connecting by exhale of something inner to another, simply sharing what we do not notice, a sleepy brilliance, awareness long forgotten.

Yet, light within does not wither. But shaded by shadows, absorbed through hurt and pain, contractions. The inner flame burns eternal, a truth, a guide, illumination of path

Awaken. Your own radiance pioneers you.

* Inspired by Rumi, The Breeze at Dawn (*Prosetry Journey*, p. 201).

In the present publication, we continue to look at different ways poetry and prose can influence each other. We also look at the diverse ways we can expand the creative efforts. For example, in our first episode, we play with collaborative writing. Instead of two people creating two separate poems or stories, we wanted to see what would happen if one person wrote the first stanza of a poem or the first paragraph of a story, then the second writer would create the next stanza or paragraph. In our experience, the writing took a different direction than either writer would have gone. And in the end, we liked the poems or stories better than if either of us would have done them by ourselves. In fact, we did the same thing writing this Introduction. We also play with rewriting each other's poem, keeping the primary idea and including aspects or related issues in the rewritten poem.

In the second episode, we play with different formats of essentially the same writing. It gives you a chance to see whether a more poetic form impacts you differently from a more prosetic design. It also provides an opportunity to examine if one design or another elicits other feelings or emotions. The third episode provides a diverse set of prosetry examples, which may stimulate you to try using this form with your own writing.

The fourth episode includes primarily short stories. Even here, we try to include more poetic descriptions and expressions to describe and share the surroundings, people, and events. In this way, poetry and prose influences each other to touch the reader and enliven the story. This episode contains two abecedarian poems, a form that uses the letters of the alphabet in order, with each line or verse beginning with a successive letter. It also includes a found prosetry piece, and two collaborative stories, Childhood and Crossroads. We encourage you to explore such a course of creation with another writer with whom you feel some affinity.

After Marianne experienced being trapped with her husband in a foreign hotel during a revolt around them, it became clear how useful and important writing can be in times of terror. These poems formed the foundation for our "Resilience in Times of Terror" episode, where we also included a few colleagues to share some of their experiences and Geoffrey reflected one of his own challenging experiences.

In the last three episodes, we explore writing poetry and prosetry related to art, writing a piece where the words also suggest some artistic form, and using music as inspiration for prosetry or poetry. Each is slightly different, but always using some other art form as a collaboration with the expression in words. Such inspiration alternatives simply expand the possibilities of where we source ideas and themes for our writing.

Most importantly, we hope this volumn encourages your own expression through these or other types of creativity and move outside traditional forms where it feels appropriate or necessary. We also hope you enjoy what we and our colleagues have shared here that may in some form nudge your creative efforts and push your work in a direction that excites your and illucits expression in your own manner.

1st Episode
Playing with Poetry

*If you don't tell the truth about yourself,
you can't tell it about other people.*

— **Virginia Wolf**

Questions to consider with this episode:

**What is the truth about yourself that is difficult to share?
How might you share that through poetry or prose?**

I'd Rather: A Collaborative Poem
By Geoffrey K. Leigh and Marianne Lyon

I have recently realized that I would
rather spend my precious time
with burley old wine vines
where canes can be difficult to wrap
and twist along a sturdy fruit wire
than bullying old victims who insist
that demands are compromises
then complain if they don't get their way

I shall never again contrive to stand
with soapy bucket in drive way   hose too short
too much lather   too much muss   fuss   bother
Nor will I do the self-drive through
flashing lights scream
"DRIVE FORWARD" then "GO BACK"
feel like I am under attack
I'd rather sip coffee   watch smiling crew
vacuum insides   drive her right through
she gratefully emerges all sparkly and clean

If we can create self-cleaning ovens
self-cleaning humidifiers   windows   glass
self-cleaning toilets and cat boxes
why can't we develop self-cleaning houses
where dust is absorbed when I turn on a switch
dirt never sticks to floors   rugs   furniture
while I spend time creating clever phrases
rhyming rhythms   elucidating explications
that touch the heart and tickle the funny bone

A Poetic Conversation with Dri*
By Marianne Lyon

Dri- "Marianne, my heart's desire is to shift from the lies I told myself as an adolescent. As Doc always said, 'it is not the forgetting that is crucial, but coming back to remember this truth"

Marianne- "I too have told myself lies, Dri. I never felt enough. Even now I struggle with self-love   but poetry has given my heart a voice"

Enough came to me
been too tired to seek her lately
but she found me

                    Enough came to me
              understood   I had come through
                  succeeded   survived
                more whole than before

                I had hoped to know her
                    dreamed of her
                    now she is here
      She says "I need to go soon   You are enough"

I say, "I'm afraid that I won't know what enough is"

            She says "Say only enough words
              think only enough thoughts,
              walk only enough walks,
              sing only enough songs,
            LOVE only enough people"

        I say,   "Please stay and walk with me"

And she says, "You have an enough guide
inside of you,
trust her with all your heart"

"She is the sister to the voices all woman have
and must embrace before any other voice"

"Smile, listen, breathe   feel   feel deep   deeper yet
You know all the answers to enoughness

*Inspired by the protagonist in the novel, *Dancing with Audacity* and a primary character in *The Catalyst Coalition*, both by Geoffrey K. Leigh.

After Loneliness Takes Its Final Bow
By Marianne Lyon

I will stop inventing stories
stop forcing them on others   making the world
a reason for my pain   painting pictures
with morbid colors of my isolation
entitling the collection   *does anything matter*

This morning   something gives way
including my wicked desire to make everyone
unlinked   detached   separate
I feel like I am dropped onto a
solitary mountain cliff   way below   a valley
where you all are   his sonorous echo
invites me into the oneness vale

And then   the way a boulder weary of clinging
rolls into a fertile hollow
I start to plunge down into abundant field
thick with wild cucumber   miner's lettuce
Oh! the fragrant blue elderberry
I am gifted one bloom at a time
In all your tearstained faces I see
rotating casts of forgotten   forsaken
so many odes of acidic desolation

Yet   you all continue to offer me florets
He bids me improvise an offering bouquet
lay it at shoeless feet of loneliness
touch her outstretched palms
listen from deep-set eyes

maybe it was your sainted invocations
maybe   a collective plot
maybe it was supernatural stare of resting raven
maybe the right time in my evolution
but loneliness   yes   loneliness has a voice
smiles   he gestures you all closer to me
you caress me   loneliness pontificates
two sentences that may take a life time to unravel

*What makes us lonely may be different,
where it hurts is always the same.* Quote attributed to Carl Jung.

Awakening
Geoffrey K. Leigh

If I were a healthy vine
with stout shaggy gray trunk
bright green leaves absorbing sunlight
I would expend my early growth
transforming buds to promising blossoms
flowers to minuscule green donations that
swell   mature   veraison to purple
spend days amping my sweet development
at night restful   brace for morrow's exertion
a gradual ripen   day after week after month
prepping for the autumn cluster collection
readying to release my plump offspring
then encourage yeast to morph progeny
into bountiful potion when process completes
with my year's work accomplished
as the product of my toil ages
softens   balances   matures
with later transfer for available offering

Winter initiates my restoration
when water refreshes during dormancy
my roots reach deep   forage
embrace soil in quest for nutrients
from planted ground cover between cordons
below the surface seeking sustaining assistance
waiting for the vine loving stewards
brawny hands grip tight their shears
in sludge from heavy winter rains
that seize boots pruners nearly lose

as they analyze past expansion
remove unneeded growth that diverts nutrients
leave promising bright buds   ready the new
anticipating the coming year
and the one after that
trimming away that not useful
helping with removal I can't do myself
allow my new developments to spring forth
for my progeny manifests from the nutriments
readying me for an additional year
then another   40 to 50 in a good life
of giving annual bounty anew
and dispensing it eventually with
those seeking magic when lovingly shared

I Am the Branch*
By Marianne Lyon

I am fruited branch
lilt like awakened woman
belly-dancing under tent in faraway desert
palms lift   arms undulate
flow effortlessly in rhythmic morning breeze

He is healthy vine
drops of water drip
like jewels
delicate rivers of glisten
undulate beneath him
Given water unselfishly
like the woman at the well
he accepts nourishment
coolness washes his feet
sinks into his roots and

I sprout from him
was imagined
before he was planted
and together
we bring into being miracle fruit
plump offerings from migrants
gifts for the drinkers of wine

What would it be
to feel rooted in rich soil
fed
tended
loved

and only need to let
our leafy arms grow
Only give back
the fruit
of who we are

*Based on John 15:5, New Testament
A rewriting of Awakening by Geoffrey K. Leigh

New Eyes
By Marianne Lyon

I'm devastated
yet the world is unrelentingly
filled with goodness

Weaving around error
fear   dread
is faithful moon
rising each night
in her fuzzy white gauze veil

Is the young waitress
who made of her body a circle
to embrace with her love my pain.

Is the laugher
of my husband next to me.

Is the faithful sun
finding holes in the clouds
then slips through the window
to sit on the floor

And I feel myself bloom
like a daffodil
grateful to be touched
by moon   sun   embrace   laughter
I feel my eyes open   nudged to see
how everything is holy

Sentience: After *New Eyes* by Marianne Lyon
Geoffrey K. Leigh

Two seemingly contradictory positions
Touch and impact in variegated manner
First one   then another   possibly a third
Spinning wildly around my view
And my innards in apparent same moment

Devastation and unrelentingly goodness
Error fear dread and full moon
Graced by fluffy white gauze veil
My pain and young circled embracing love

Presently one appears greater
Later overshadowed by another
Back and forth in whirlwind experience
Overwhelmed   fleeting   one or opposite
Unclear which may dominate next

Husband's laughter next to me
Faithful sun finding cloud's holes
Until collective blooms me like daffodil
And eyes open to holiness of all

As I slow the mixing of elements
Step back to focus my new vision
One more option manifests the aggregate
Where I allow and embrace my chosen prospect
Of what matters most in this school of life

Another Poetic Conversation with Dri*
By Marianne Lyon

Marianne : "Dri, I am so intrigued with your memories about your work with Doc and your amazing marriage to Tiago. What are your thoughts about the gifts of life esp. marriage?

Dri: " Marianne rather than just telling I would love to write a collative poem about our married lives   you with Jim and of course my dear life with Tiago"

> M: Who doesn't remember
> Their first kiss and who
> Doesn't remember the
> Burst like a sparkler
> Into every part of yourself
>
> Dri: Tiago eyes orbit my face
> Clear as a morning lake
> And of course his gentle smile
> Begging permission to lean in
> And let speechless lips
> Soak in wild happiness
>
> M: Who doesn't remember
> Asking why the first shy glance
> Giddy stroll on rocky beach
> A brush of fingers would
> Lead to raptured communion

Dri: Marianne what do you think about the notion of Silent Love? Sometimes words can't express my quiet love that dances between Tiago and myself. Is there a quiet love between you and Jim?

M: There is all around

Whirling world of silent love
Everywhere I look
His quiet   merciful hands touch
Heal   reach for
Companioned walk at dusk

D: if I become quiet
enough   I am able to
Feel rhythmic voice of his heart
Tiago's love joyously unraveling
In pungent quiet

Marianne: I love our poetry conversations Dri   more please soon.

*Inspired by the protagonist in the novel, *Dancing with Audacity* and a primary character in *The Catalyst Coalition*, both by Geoffrey K. Leigh.

*I have never started a poem yet whose end I knew.
Writing a poem is discovering*

— **Robert Frost**

**Want to take a few minutes and respond to Frost's quote?
Or something else in this Episode?**

2nd Episode
Juxtapose Form and Feeling

I would define, in brief, the poetry of words as the rhythmical creation of beauty.

— Edgar Allen Poe

Questions to consider with this episode:

**Was there a time when you heart felt weightless?
How does your heart converse with you about creativity?**

So Many Roads to the Watering Hole*
By Marianne Lyon

The plane cruises low.
Human imprint visible
thatched huts   makeshift fences
geometry of agriculture

Sun creates a sparkle
spits sparks at me from
slithering blue serpentine river

Pilot changes course
over rust-colored desert
Eyes fix on one thin road
then hundreds of others
Shrubs like tufts of hair
edge their winding
I see his grey lumbering
ears wave, trunk sways
He is a feast of motion

We circle down
His chosen path
cuts narrow then widens
Ahead sun glints a diamond
He reaches edge of watering hole
From that mecca
other empty paths spread
like rays a child draws from a sun

Was it a map that led him there
or perhaps memory

Once long ago or every year
in African sun   when rain
stops its plummeting
does he walk this same road
feeling joy   thirst quenched

Plane roars on
I feel ground and sky
pulse with his presence
Finding a path is easy
if you know the way

* Inspired by an Elephant in Botswana

Speak From The Heart
By Geoffrey K. Leigh

Anything essential that yearns to be expressed emanates best through the heart. Far too frequently, contrivances become taxonomized purely from the head.

Allow wisdom of the cardiac organ to suffuse emotional elements that hold expanse for concepts to be digested. Not just through thought, words, but space and energy. Facilitate greater elucidation.

If I say to you, look at the difference in the shades of green on this tree compared to that. You notice a distinction. If I instead point out that shorter days unmask and display a leaf's diverse, underlying chemical colors. Consider such contrast.

When hearts protect, comments roil the atmosphere.

Before we continue conversations, release the covering. Relax our reflexive fortifications. Let the heart breathe. Exercise expansion. Then share your truth on love's wings.

Speak From The Heart

Anything essential
that yearns to be expressed
emanates best through the heart
Far too frequently
contrivances become taxonomized
purely from the head

Allow wisdom
of the cardiac organ
to suffuse emotional elements
that hold expance
for concepts to be digested
Not just through thought   words
but space and energy
facilitate greater elucidation

If I say to you
look at the difference
in the shades of green
on this tree
compared to that
you notice a distinction
If I instead point out
that shorter days
unmask and display
the leaf's diverse
underlying chemical colors
Consider such a contrast

When hearts protect
comments roil the atmosphere

Before we continue conversations
release the covering
relax our reflexive fortifications
let the heart breathe
exercise expansion
then share your truth
on love's wings

An Unenvisioned Gem
By Geoffrey K. Leigh

My heart.

My broken heart, my longing heart, follow my heart, heart to heart.

My heart's desire.

Since boyhood, my heart did not always belong to me. Oft given to others in exchange for hopes of an enduring connection. Bestow my love and self to another, wanting to forge a lasting intimate relationship. In the process, I give up myself. Anything to be appreciated, loved.

I initiate self abandon, then spawn anger for the outcome. Sometimes from a minor infraction. A focused indignation at other when I initiated the abdication. Many contrasts in rhythm, melody and harmony. All variations of a common theme.

Each time, an ending. Each time, a failure. Repeatedly followed by deep sorrow in my cavernous chest.

Self desertion as offer for lasting love. An uneven trade. A tragedy. At the time, an apparent essential.

Subsequently, bereavement randomly reappears. From a song, a memory flash, a glance from a stranger's eye. Something here. Another there. All reminds of losing the coveted outcome.

The antithesis belies irritation for such unobtainable fantasy, dream, hallucination, mirage. Why such a perpetuated ideal if not available for all? Is it me? Am I the only one to repeatedly reach and lose? Why clutch such illusion when the result stimulates irritation?

Anger generated for conception of such chimera, obtained by others and always just beyond my reach. The myths, books, movies all tell such tales. I bought them and believed.

With constant focus on external vision, internal blossoms and gifts ignored. Such aspects labeled minor, unimportant. With emphasis on unobtainable dream, inner exploration became ostracized. Why waste time and energy on interior work when exterior qualities viewed most attractive, valued? I prioritized the most significant asset, external connection.

Rumi counseled in The Bright Core of Failure:

Sometimes you enter the heart.
Sometimes you are born from the soul.
Sometimes you weep a song of separation.
It is all the same glory.

Even if they find nothing but ruins
and failure, you are the bright core of that.

Devoid of an intimate external relationship, locus morphs to available moldable territory. Emphasize procurable works. Fashion modifications where one can enable influence.

I dig. Explore. Learn. Search dark crevices. I shine supplemental light on hidden hurts. I scour and polish. I interrogate my belief of not being enough, wounds becoming tonnages that pull at my joy, diminish my life spark, hurt my heart.

My cavernous hiding places brighten. I initiate increasing release of weights, nightmares, disappointments, shame. The emancipation frees me from the density of my body, liberating my essence. Piece by piece, measure by measure. The cleansing begins to lighten my body. My being. My heart.

My vision of self expands. My dreams inclusive of whole self, outer and inner. My hurt lessens without complete evaporation. World view enlarges with meaningful aspects previously ignored. My life begins to rejoice by including both pain and joy. Sadness and satisfaction. Wound and wonder.

The flash still evokes images of the dream, my yearning. Yet, increasingly the present song includes light with dark, jazz with blues, and fresh mustard fragrance among dormant vines.

I habit embracement of inner euphoria that at times now can chuckle at the everlasting fantasy.

A poem in response to *An Unenvisioned Gem*
By Marianne Lyon

Ah, but I was so much older then
I'm younger than that now – Bob Dylan

I wish to see
with child eyes
be   bedazzled
not bewildered   bitter
converse with birds
that flutter overhead
ditty-dance around
pine trees
collect magical
copper ore
scattered
on baron hills
want to see right into
the center of things
glittering   bursting
episodes that never stop
dreams that come true
not listen to mysterious force
that tells me it is impossible
I want to harness grins
cause belly laughs   howls
my hands wild windmill pumping
joy for all to catch
back then   I dreamed
of those moments
I know that because I can

go there   right now
small hands   dinky feet
tingle with delight
even when pain pounded
did not feel enough
I pleaded to understand
how wide my young self was
how fanciful   joyous
inquisitive
Now   aged
I feel this authentic wish
born like a new morn
today   proudly
coming true

Light
By Geoffrey K. Leigh

A light glows

just beyond our physical focus
ever present   gently waiting
a subtle unflappable flame
to devour our doubts   fears   pain

I felt it as a child

connection and support   love
I experienced her overwhelm
an adolescent in search of truth
clarity of vision and understanding
one night so open   I surrender
yet lacking context to imbed
deeper possibilities

Without an idea of how to hold it

I bypassed the opportunity
it didn't make me a better player
student   stalwart leader   confident friend
for it lights from the inside
a dark unfamiliar place
the hole I refuse to explore
the pain and hurt I divert and cover

I find a door

later in my explorations
unlocked these many years

allowing a vision and experience
of this patient presence
wishing I understood its benefaction
as a child or emerging adult
to live from this light all along

Light

A light glows just beyond our physical focus, ever present
gently waiting, a subtle unflappable flame
to devour our doubts, fears and pain

I felt it as a child, connection and support, love
I experienced her overwhelm, an adolescent in search of truth
clarity of vision and understanding, one night so open I surrender
yet lacking context to imbed deeper possibilities

Without an idea of how to hold it, I bypassed the opportunity
it didn't make me a better player, student, stalwart leader or confident friend
for it lights from the inside, a dark unfamiliar place
the hole I refuse to explore, the pain and hurt I divert and cover

I find a door later in my explorations, unlocked these many years
allowing a vision and experience of this patient presence
wishing I understood its benefaction as a child or emerging adult
to live from this light all along

Creativity is a wild mind and a disciplined eye.

— Dorothy Parker

Powers
By Geoffrey K. Leigh

Flames, smoke, screams, buildings burn and people die.
What power of destruction lies within, thrust upon another?
Sometimes random, sometimes planned.
Narrow vision and focused hate, driven by anger, jealousy, contracted faith
A struggle, yet who really wins?

Birth of a new baby, seeds planted, a new memorial, construction emerges
plants flourish, hope for a future, the power of creation starts with a dream,
to build, nurture, manifest, fly, a similar process, opposing outcomes.
Step back and inhale the wonder.

Before a nightmare, a dream lingers, another potency
a nebulous option, too often blinded by driving forces,
dogma, defenses, lies, rapid reaction over heartful forethought

What if we stepped back and struggled first with the sacred power of choice?

Powers

Flames   smoke   screams
buildings burn   people die
what power of destruction
lies within   thrust upon other
sometimes random   planned
Narrow vision   focused hate
driven by anger   jealousy   contracted faith
A struggle   who really wins

Birth of a new baby   seeds planted
a new memorial
construction emerges
plants flourish   hope for a future
the power of creation starts with a dream
to build   nurture   manifest   fly
a similar process   opposing outcomes
step back   inhale the wonder

Before a nightmare   a dream
lingers another potency
a nebulous option
too often blinded by driving forces
dogma   defenses   lies
rapid reaction over heartful forethought

What if we stepped back and struggled first
with the sacred power of choice

Heritage Statues
By Geoffrey K. Leigh

Monuments and military bases
to warriors and generals
fighting against our union
A now united country
honors no other enemy
built many decades after
the civil war they represent
memories of rebellion
more importantly intimidation
against a freed race
who dare ask for impartiality
treatment as humans   compeers
encouraging an inclusion
within an original belief
All Men are Created Equal

Women now included
emigrants from other countries
races   people   orientations   identities
asking the central question
when will all mean all
when will people of all colors
genders   orientations
be included as American

Finally coming down
statue by male statue
tower by tower
a self-serving president
defends them for political gain

ignoring the masses   majority opinions
who cheer their dethroning
the towering over people
reminders of continued subjugation
finally descending to the earth
isonomy emerging in their place
while chapel bells ring out
Amazing grace

Heritage Statues

Monuments and military bases to warriors and generals fighting against
our union   A now united country honors no other enemy   representations
built many decades after the civil war they represent   memories of rebellion
more importantly intimidation against a freed race who dare ask
for impartiality treatment as humans   compeers   encouraging an inclusion
within an original belief
All Men are Created Equal

Women now included   emigrants from other countries   races   people
orientations   identities   asking the central question when will all mean all
when will people of all colors   genders   orientations
be included as full American with equal treatment and respect

Finally coming down   statue by male statue   tower by tower
a self-serving president defends them for political gain
ignoring the masses   majority opinions who cheer their dethroning
the towering over people   reminders of continued subjugation
finally descending to the earth   isonomy emerging in their place
while chapel bells ring out
Amazing grace

To My Unborn Child
By Marianne Lyon

What I want to tell you
is that you are enough
you do not have to
do anything to be loved
you do not have to perform
or achieve
or earn a merit badge
this needs to be repeated
over and over
be who you are
and love what is before you

What I want to tell you
is be courageous
be your own hero
embrace friendships
release fear   unworthiness
continue to laugh
even when you can't
remember why

What I want to tell you
is be a doggie   hell raiser
wiggling   sniffing
inquisitive   wordless
passionate for a rub
a treat   a ball-catch
not worried
about next spring

What I want to tell you
is be awake   a trailblazer
scoff illusions
that keep us believing
that what we see
in the world is gospel
that keep us from recognizing
the truth that lies
underneath

Renata*
By Geoffrey K. Leigh

She could not remember where the words first emerged or if printed on a book page long forgotten. Yet each characteristic became seared into Renata's memory. Not just some synapse in her brain. Rather, they crystalized into her essence, the core of her being. The accumulated alternative perspectives remained scattered in other parts of her brain and body, while the core ideas kept her on track.

Her mother and father loved Renata. She remained sure of that fact, although not as confidant about her older sister. At the same time, blazed into muscle tissues resided the fiery comments intended to make her a better person while burning deep into recesses of her brain.

"Don't be an idiot," remarked her father when she could not remember where she put some tools or other objects her father could not find.

"You'll amount to nothing if you don't work harder in school," screeched her mother when Renata received anything less than an A grade.

"You couldn't carry a tune if I gave you a wheelbarrow," jabbered her sister whenever Renata began to sing one of her numerous favorite songs.

"You'll never be a singer with that voice," pronounced her choir teacher after she got so nervous her voiced cracked on a solo.

From somewhere deep inside, her grandma's comments over voiced the more immediate family and school perspectives. She spent many summers with her maternal grandmother, who shared her unwavering support and clarity. This unwavering melody frequently reminded Renata that she did not have to do anything, perform in a particular way, or excel at something to be loved by this open hearted sage.

"Simply be the bright light that you are," she kept telling young Renata. This young girl's heart expanded every time she considered the loving words.

Despite the comments intended for improvement by immediate family, teachers or school mates, Renata felt a determination in her core to do what she wanted most: express her joy of life through piano and vocal music. She also believed there was a better way to raise a child, if, in her unwavering view, she had the good fortune to bear one.

As she grew, Renata sang quietly alone in her bedroom, the shower, on long walks, and when she danced behind closed bedroom doors. After much persistence, her parents allowed her to take piano lessons if she practiced when no one remained at home. Given the heavy parental involvement in work and her sister's participation with school and social activities, this aspiring artist found time to play in the otherwise empty house.

At college, Renata studied music and practiced daily. She thrived in her child development and family system classes. But the classes that surprised her the most were the English courses that focused on poetry. She never considered the close connection between poetry, short stories and song lyrics until she explored all three with earnest. The complimentary styles excited her to do more contrasting forms, especially when composing a new song.

In those moments, writing lyrics, a story or poetry, she felt closest to the shining light of her core. Words emerged on the page from some place deep inside. She never questioned the source and trusted the manifestation.

One spring day during her final semester, she decided to take a walk around campus. The trees exposed their full blossoms, as did the many bushes and wild flowers. When she walked, shoes clutched the ground as if a steadfast connection occurred each time her foot touched the earth. She found a warm bench with the sun at her back and watched students enjoying the snugness of the sun and fresh air.

She noticed several couples sitting on other benches around the square or lying on blankets in the grass. One man was sitting directly on the grass with a woman's head in his lap. The man was stroking the woman's long brown hair with his other hand cupped between her face and his pants. On the sidewalk near this couple, a man was pushing a stroller filled with a small sleeping child while the woman's arm encircled his.

Renata pulled out her notebook and began to write. She remained unsure in the beginning whether the words were lyrics, a story or a poem. She simply continued to write. The words rang true as she created loving inspiration for her own, unborn child.

* Inspired by Marianne Lyon's poem, *To My Unborn Child*.

Consequential Expression
By Geoffrey K. Leigh

Life from the head   a comfortable location
except to express experiences that contain consequential elucidation
utterances that convey love   grief   joy   heartache

When I employ words for such potent occasions
they derive from my heart
I begin an essential message that carries myself in written meaning
allows my concentrated words to soar in the breeze
while breath serves love to my soul

Consequential Expression

Life from the head
a comfortable location
except to express
experiences that contain
consequential elucidation
conveying love   grief
joy   heartache

When I employ words
for potent occasions
they derive from the heart
to begin an essential message
that carries myself
in written meaning
allow my concentrated words
to sour in the breeze
while breath
serves love to my soul

Pride
By Geoffrey K. Leigh

A human sounds   acts   talks
likes   looks   loves
in ways contrasting your expected
manners   behaviors   desires

What inner discomfort arises
What fear gets triggered
What animosity darkens
your openness and heart

Before allowing your darkness
to turn into hate and hurt
ask what may be overlooked
in your inner environs

How does your light darken
turn destructive
your own affect transform
from love to lynching

And in that contracted reaction
where does your light hide
your own love disappear
one's heart collapsed in a landslide of muck

What if the force of change
began inside   clearing our debris first
brightening our heart's light
to shine joy on all the colorful flowers

Pride

A human sounds, acts, talks, likes, looks, loves
in ways contrasting your expected manners, behaviors and desires.

What inner discomfort arises, what fear gets triggered
What animosity darkens your openness and heart

Before allowing your darkness to turn into hate and hurt
ask what may be overlooked in your inner environs

How does your light darken, turn destructive
your own love transform from love to lynching

And in that contracted reaction, where does your light hide
your own love disappear, one's heart collapsed in a landslide of muck

What if the force of change began inside, clearing our debris first
brightening our heart's light to shine joy on all the colorful flowers

Dawn
By Geoffrey K. Leigh

Light beams peek
over Stag's Leap
illuminate clouds
budding vineyards
obtrude through
slits in blind
top of curtain
irradiate cream wall
black picture frame
eyes faintly ajar
heart at rest
breath suspires
in natural fluctuation

Am I truly alive
if I do not
do
produce
achieve
assist
share
save
move

If alive
more to do
or not do
being
choosing
creating

Mind stretches to observe
early opening of day
overflow of possibilities
await my options
choices
volition of decisions

Or possibly more slumber

Dawn

Light beams peek over Stag's Leap   illuminate clouds, budding vineyards
obtrude through slits in blind   top of curtain
irradiate cream wall   black picture frame
eyes faintly ajar   heart at rest   breath suspires in natural fluctuation

Am I truly alive if I do not do   produce   achieve   assist   share   save   move
If alive   more to do or not do   being   choosing   creating

Mind stretches to observe early opening of day   overflow of possibilities
await my options   choices   volition of decisions

Or possibly more slumber

*Risala** to Rumi
By Geoffrey K. Leigh

Your words transpose notes
that awaken the silence
into timeless melodies and riffs
that nourish my core light
Even when I cannot see or feel
I know the brightness of light's dawn
through your melodic insight
as its vastness of ardor embraces
all the sorrow and pain
with a caress of smitten sounds
that soothe and heal

When I forget   you share images
that help me member
then remember time and again
for once experienced and internalized
their force continues to extend
to the outer reaches of my consciousness
then soothe my pain and doubt
as a salve to my soul
showing strength in vulnerability
extending permission for a loving
change of focus that heals all wounds

With the reparative sustenance
emerges many forms of gratitude and elegance
for the vision and affection shared
through harmonic images and messages
releasing such love   such vision
that one's core shines as brilliant

as the sun on a summer's afternoon
and fills every cell of one's being
in ways that only inner eyes
can behold the power, the beauty
of one's naked core radiance

**Risala* means "message, epistle" in Arabic

*Risala** to Rumi

Your words transpose notes that awaken the silence
into timeless melodies and riffs that nourish my core light
Even when I cannot see or feel   I know the brightness
of light's dawn through your melodic insight
as its vastness of ardor embraces all the sorrow and pain
with a caress of smitten sounds that soothe and heal

When I forget   you share images that help me member then remember
time and again   for once experienced and internalized
their force continues to extend to the outer reaches of my consciousness
then soothe my pain and doubt as a salve to my soul
showing strength in vulnerability   extending permission
for a loving change of focus that heals all wounds

With the reparative sustenance emerges many forms of gratitude and elegance
for the vision and affection shared through harmonic images and messages
releasing such love   such vision that one's core shines as brilliant
as the sun on a summer's afternoon and fills every cell of one's being
in ways that only inner eyes can behold the power   the beauty
of one's naked core radiance

* *Risala* means "message, epistle" in Arabic

The worst enemy to creativity is self-doubt.

— Sylvia Plath

A question to consider with your writing:

Flick through this chapter.
Is there a line which resonates you?
Use that as your starting point and carry on from there.

3rd Episode
Prosetry

*Poetry is the lifeblood of rebellion, revolution,
and the rising of consciousness.*

— Alice Walker

A question to consider during this episode:

**Envision a unique poetry form.
What might it look or sound like?**

Envision and Scheme*
By Geoffrey K. Leigh

Imagine what your world would be like if you heard flowers blossom, not only on beautiful days, but when dark with pain, conflict, and war. What if you felt beauty bursting forth irregardless of what occurs, determined to illicit elements of elegance in every sphere of your life?

Fantasize oaks as they express messages of centurial wisdom, elucidating how roots dig deeply, allowing a sway in the breeze without a shift in their stance. The leaves whisper fantasies and visions of transforming sunlight into corporeal energetics, verdant green lusciousness everywhere you settle a glance.

Visualize grapes prospering in vineyards, each varietal exposing luxurious color and liquid, waiting patiently to slip into a tank for processing its mature flavor. Varietals lack competition between grapes, rather aspire to burst fragrant scent, taste that stimulates savoring, a lengthy finish to appreciate its gift to the palate.

Envision the transformation from grape to succulent nectar, fermenting its best without concern about the ambrosia of other varietals or vintages, focused on the best possible nose and palate, enticing piquancies to enhance the setting, interaction, connection occurring with those imbibing the bountiful bouquet.

Project, as a part of nature, your dream rather than what you hide and avoid, only recognizing your hidden masks on other faces. Unleash the vulnerability to live an authentic life, wasting no energy to hide, compare, pretend, or energize illusions that distract from your organic essence.

Conceive others' genuine nature, seeing through their masks, avoid attributing your transmutations, covering contributions made from another heart. Are there truly differences to adjudicate, separate, and determine relative worth when the whole composes all parts, creating something grander than ingredients?

Hallucinate a world where hearts are wide open, when people care as deeply for others as they do for their own persona. Where people care as much

for themselves as they do others, for sometimes it is steelier to bring
the love inside rather than allowing it to embrace external beings.

Scheme and endeavor to allow hearts to blossom, express love within, between,
with no barriers to twist and suffocate the gifts it bears, extending its energy
to include the source that holds and nurtures it, sharing undistorted love,
vitality, connecting us with the magnificence that abides all around

* Inspired by Simone de Beauvoir: "One's life has value so long as one attributes
value to the life of others, by means of love, friendship, indignation, compassion."

Dared*
By Marianne Lyon

*Sometimes you spill your fears into the room and there is no place on earth then more holy as your words unfurl like curls of incense in fractaled unspiraling, each sob, each murmur a tendril of smoke I follow until it disappears. How I treasure these times when you let me meet all of you. When I leave, I look the same, the scent of trust clinging to my skin. But I am rearranged within.***

If I dream of embarking on a water quest, I would choose a wooden canoe, that slides from shore with just strong nudging. Bid farewell to worried faces, hope they see yearning that aches from my eyes. I invite Sacagawea be my companion. Our hearts stretch tout to vast liquid distance that opens instant by instant to that which bids us embark.

She instructs me surrender to waves of unknown adversity. Loamy cadences begin to liniment regretful fears. Salty wind carries gentle fragrance of freedom when suddenly panic needles when no oars appear in her hands nor in mine, but she calmly whispers—listen, and when my breathing returns I begin to hear canoe hum cello harmonies with gentle billows courageously trumpet discords at surging pillars.

Magically, canoe joins orbit of dolphins. Brushes dwarfed island shore, ruckus with chirping chicks. Canoe doesn't seem to mind that our hands are free to trace buttery morning sunlight or touch sun-spangled swells numbingly cold. Doesn't seem to care that our eyes aren't fixed on beaches alight with bond fires or packed with screaming children flying kites.

Memories flicker back to my tempest land-life lurking with unending plans mindless doing, keeping promises, seeking always a safety net.
If I desire a water quest, I will choose a wooden canoe, engage Sacagawea's company purposely leave the oars behind.

* A sense of courage, audacity, or willingness to take risks in the face of adversity.
** Rosemary Wahtola Trommer poem - *Trust*

I Am Solid
By Geoffrey K. Leigh

I am rock solid, which then crumbles as sands shift from waves of change
rolling towards shore as I search the sad eyes of old woman begging for a dollar.
I feel support by people who view me favorably and applaud my efforts
until we disagree, fighting over perspectives, what is right or not.
I am solid in the way I view the world, defining bad or good, until I include a
different angle of how judgments hurt others or disregard another's experience.
I am worthy of earning money by made contributions, as long as I ignore
how my work undermines other's health, safety, or livelihood.

Physicists inform, molecules contain more space than matter,
which makes me wonder if anything or anyone is solid, sure, certain.
I search for some thing, idea, dogma, revelation, anything that would
provide some sense of unyielding with heart ajar.

As I continue in breath, I question my need for foundation upon which to stand,
firm, fixed, resolute, strong.
What I learned as a child may not be true?
That sturdy dogma to steady my walk was temporary?

I breathe again, notice and feel into extending and collapsing lungs,
which provide life's flowing oxygen.
I put my hand to my heart, pay attention to the beat, beat, expanding
and contracting beat that spreads living liquid to every organ of my body.
Sometimes I am supportive of others and, at other times, I hurt people
with my words expressed through angry breath.
Maybe when I notice, feel, clear blinders from my eyes, and hear others cry
my experience of expanding after contractions is my foundational strength.

Beginnings
By Geoffrey K. Leigh

An initial moment of galactic creativity, when all that exists is chaos and possibility, vague thought still illusive, spiraling at the edge of consciousness wanting to emerge into manifestation, waiting to take form, yet unorganized, potential and power without focus, embryonic and unrealized.

Possibility transforms into a blueprint, emanates intention as configuration. Design manifests, not always exactly as envisioned, sometimes elated, other times heartbreak. Sometimes a harmonic shift, other times discordant, modulating keys, tempo to a fabrication that can excite or disappoint.

A budding song, story, relationship, home, expressing elation, passion, a creative process unfolding piece by piece, interactions and patterns, bits, segments come together, transform chaos into structured composition to convey an idea, visioned structure, symphony, love letter, heart connection.

In the afterwards, do creations impact originators, change begetter foundations with interactions between possibility and product? Intention and articulation? Once notes turn to song, words to story, trees to homes, names to connections, will body, brain, heart stay the same? Does creativity actualize metamorphosis?

Experiencing inspired process can open one to the place of innovation, artistry, access of ideas, flow of imagination, an innovative connection of words, segments that inspire the creator and consumer. A gift, blessing to builder and inhabitant. Might such innovative practices invite one to the experience an all knowing state?

Who Am I?
By Geoffrey K. Leigh

Assessment most obvious considers physical size, color, sex, gender, weight, looks. easy to assess, prime aspects to adjudicate by others and self.

Labels for connection oft encompassed in identity and emotional share exchange as child, friend, neighbor, spouse, lover, parent, grandparent.

Life tasks undertaken provide diverse experiences, adventures, yearnings from student to teacher, researcher to writer, musician to conductor, hermit to host.

Various roles, pains and excitement, related or new journeys that wane and wax as decisions and circumstances impact explorations, desires, drives, passions.

Each search stimulates challenges, excitement, prowess, proficiencies, increase of skills and competence, discharge interferences, exonerate hurts and wounds.

New dimensions add expanded abilities, sentiments, bruises. Previous qualities released? Replaced? Yet unused muscles atrophy, unwatered flowers die.

What drives motivation for change, adventure? What encourages creation? Where lies desire to apply diverse forms that radiate priorities and principles?

At the penetralia shines a light that directs motivation, origination. A clearly radiating flame? No longer darkened under defenses? A crystalline illumination?

My Inner Song
By Marianne Lyon

Perhaps you, too, have heard it, despite the cacophony,
a song that rises in you—a tune you've never learned
that somehow owns you the way white owns winter,
the way breath owns our lives. Perhaps you, too,
have marveled as the tune spills forward, guiding you,
keeping you company so that even when alone,
you know for certain you are not alone. *

Life-other-than-my–own runs-through-me **

My walking path calls me almost every morning to same hidden spot   same slight bend behind statued oak a smell of jasmine whiffs me to Grandma's yard   She welcomes me with sweeping arms   wraps around my surrendering self   in that moment of cares   I step out of her springtime embrace   love her back with a smile   like a sunrise her old all- knowing eyes are a

never-stop-soothing-honey-for-my-tender-heart.

I walk further exhilarated on my adventure path   gravel floor laced with tree shadows that save me from burning sun   am inspired to call these shapes

cool-angels-that-hover-without-anywhere else-to-be.

As if their leafy wings flutter a rhythm   a song dances in me   a song threaded in hope   Can't remember all the words   but I softly hum and the beckoning vibration is like

a-warm-hand-pulling-me-from-a deep-well

I keep walking   breathing the calm melody   grateful for my feet stepping me grateful for Native American's way of naming lifelong   moments   of life that have a-life-other-than-my-own that-runs-through-me.

Inspired by:
* Poem by Rosemary Wahtola Trommer
** Mark Nepo- Utterance-that Rises-Briefly-From-The Source

Even As We Dance*
By Geoffrey K. Leigh

Religion predetermined my childhood foundation, by good-intentioned parents, with generations of ancestral heritage and legendary sacrifices in regnant church. Bearing children remained a mixture of God-like responsibility and duty, without succumbing to filthy fleshy pleasures.
One could procreate with great reverence, even donning sacred clothing, but I was religioned not to enjoy the passion of creation.

Slow dancing was allowed with specified distance between woman and man, but rock n roll forbidden, for fear of propagating lascivious and lewd behaviors.

Growing older, I chose unreligioned acts that included carnal interactions and bodily system revelry, like our ardent affinities.
I began to procreate revolutionary questions: If creation is a god-like act, why would connective interaction with accompanying ebulliences engage evil?
Worse: If my physical being is the result of a god-like act, why am I not inherently a mini-he/she/they?

In the end, the answer that formed trusts pleasure with our corporeal connection, a reverent sense of authentic love that erupts between us, even as we dance.

Inspired by Julia Childs' saying: "A party without cake is just a meeting," and a conversation about dancing with Marianne Lyon.

A poet is, before anything else, a person who is passionately in love with language.

— **W. H. Arden**

New Explorations
By Geoffrey K. Leigh

Want to climb cathedral steps in Florence	*Been there*
Explore the Eiffel Tower	*Done that*
Wine taste in Spain	*There too*
Hike around Edinburgh	*Accomplished*
Play on the shores of Sydney	*Enjoyable*
Hear vibrations in Cairo's pyramids	*Astounding*
Stroll the garden of dreams in Kathmandu	*Tranquil*
Experience the world of Seoul	*Impressive*
Treasure the architecture of St. Petersburg	*Intricate*
Savor a Stargazy pie from Cornwall	*Yep*
Create something never imagined	*What?*
Write a story no one's conceived	*Impossible*
Trust your creative juices	*Wait a minute*
Overcome creative resistance	*What's that*
Dance on a feather in water	*Inconceivable*
Sit in sublime	*Ah . . . well*
Nurture innovation	*Maybe*
Allow gratitude to overwhelm you	*How*
Limn the joys of life	*Is that possible*
Love who you are	*Does anyone*

Worldly adventures appear easily
As focus remains beyond self
The inner landscape less obvious, subtle
Yet there lie creative adventures
Always available, accessible
With novel perspectives, untapped potentialities
What fires the inner spark
Invigorates recesses of creativity
Illuminates untaped gifts

And inspires inner expression from essence   *Hum*

How
By Geoffrey K. Leigh

How can imagination expand to paint, express, mold, dance
to inspire, envision, create, share like no one else

How might brain, eyes, hands, heart expand to possibilities
others could not allow themselves to unfold

How could one manifest creation that becomes unique, magnificent
when no previous being could caress the canvas or play on paper
fly across the floor, construct with clay or stone
such visions escaped those before them, now lost in the multiverse

How does the magical creative expression emerge
open to places and sources beyond one letter, step, stroke at a time
hands in clay or pen on parchment while head reaches for clouds
and heart expands beyond the chest, touching something galvanic

May such magic permeate arts and science
forging new frontiers from a place once viewed ordinary

May the muse touch head, hand and heart
for creation to flow freely and manifest a world previously unforeseen

Possibility
By Geoffrey K. Leigh

If I cut your body with a razor, you hurt, bleed, focus full attention on the wound.
You summon help of a surgeon, clean, wrap, repair damage with minimal scar.
Your body knows a healing process, experienced surgeons diminish evidence.
You begin healing the moment of the cut, medical resources make you whole.

If I don't want your scar to show, I use a much more subtle instrument.
I cut your self-worth with words sharp as the Damascus sword,
tearing at the sense of who you are and any available alternatives,
slicing you one word at a time
again, and again, and again, and again
until little remains, including any evidentiary scar.

Cuts with a razor can leave scar badges of honor and determination to survive.
Word cuts may not allow even you to identify where to begin repairs or realize
the damage. They leave few obvious scars to identify the savage attack.
Worst of all, they stimulate your creative cover that conceals any light within.

If I choose your harm to increase my sense of value, word cuts reign supreme.
They hide the evidence and reflect responsibility back to you.
But I first must incise out of myself any care or concern.
My own defense armoring of heart requires solidification and complete isolation.

If instead, my word slicing intends a removal of your heart defense,
I first must eliminate my own protections, open myself to new possibilities.
Any cuts now require strategic insertion in places less noticeable.
Sliding words and expanded perspectives repeatedly until you cease to defend,
not against me, your perceived enemy, rather from your unimagined nightmare:
the truth of who you really are.

The first element in creation of loving radiance is caressing alternative options,
care, nurture, perspective, delicate embracement of hope in feathery hands.

For whatever has the nature of ceasing has the nature of arising, including inner luminosity. Choose your option of inner essence wisely.

Nonsense and Sense
By Geoffrey K. Leigh

How do I understand one person's sense that appears as nonsense?
Can you explore me a foundation where I recognize the substance?
What do I miss and where do I strike light into this murkiness?
I love the playfulness, yet how do I recognize the play?

A rose is a rose is a rock is a raspberry
I cower before the insight that escapes my understanding
Possibly if I language my life sufficiently
I will perceive a world I never before imagined

Yet my mind feels trapped inside a finite brain
Continuous random rattles rather than new neural pathways
Limited connections within infinite possibilities
Screaming to break free with no sound in sight

Alas, I suspire to unwind my twisted reasoning
Unbar the finite, allowing vast prospects to appear
That I might embrace unforeseen opportunities
Never before imagined in my enclosed existence.

Categories
By Geoffrey K. Leigh

Growing up, adults dichotomized my world: black or white, democracy or communism, male or female, young or old, science or mysticism, straight or gay.

Eventually, my color palette incorporated shades of rainbows, variations in light, governance, gender, incarnation, personal investigations, and attractions.

With increasing alternatives, unknown outcomes, anxiety increases, throwing me off balance, wanting to embrace a solid object, safely secured in a nest.

If I compress my view and hold it still, I focus sight through my life's aperture, limits in place to prevent any dissolution of my perceived truth.

If I hold tight, prevent expansion, the hardening of categories elicits safe bubble, an impermeable shell to protect me, allay my fears, and avert investigation.

An inclusive opportunity allows deep breaths, expand my life pumping organ, rejoice in the myriad miracles that await examination of unexplored possibilities.

Response to Albert*
By Geoffrey K. Leigh

If one sees only the surface, existence appears absurd, repeated habits, bipartite thought reins supreme, yet ignores corporeal and emotional information, language of the heart.

Understanding diminishes anxiety momentarily, waiting arrival of innovative questions, mutated perspectives, which reactivates consternation, apprehension.

Tension, uneasiness excludes power of choice, provokes desire for solid, mental explanations. When you assume an inverse relationship between love and absurd, limited views reign.

When love becomes existence rather than licentious living, absurd transforms to clarity. While judgments remain judgments, spirituality emanates consciousness, intangible experiences.

Love may connect, share among people, a limited experience.
Love as our existence opens us further, dispenses clarity,
dissolves the inner need for solid understanding, abandons judgment.

Arts facilitate clarity, not just of what we see, but what we overlook, ignore, miss from our vision. They help open closed perspectives and ignored life, irrespective of philosophy.

The body does shrink from annihilation, as does life's spark, continuing to lighten, if we open all our eyes to see beyond the dichotomous to streams of hued complexion.

Repose in the serenity of loving essence, from the inside out rather than the expected origination from an external source. Power of heart light within softens and cradles self.

*Inspired by The Myth of Sisyphus by Albert Camus.

An Invitation
By Geoffrey K. Leigh

A gift often shows up when I don't look   seek   search,
feel pressure to produce or manifest some product   outcome.
Instead   I attempt to expect nothing and allow an accessible position.
In that moment   I simply experience and interact with whatever appears.
Hold my heart open with no expectation. And in that nanosecond
pay attention as creation may manifest an innovative invitation.

In those moments   I observe a new light   bird nest   babbling brook
woman planting a tree   views not previously noticed or expressed
in such arrangement the experience becomes anew. I pay close attention
with unclothed eyes   remove preconceived boxes of the way
something should be   imagine rather how it might be. Remove blinders
observe with unfiltered sentiments   feel with natural eyes
view with unstructured brain   naked mind
and employ the pure power of curiosity

In that expanded space   with available love organ
I explore novel processes. Possibilities appear when open and expanded
in ways formerly unattempted   unallowed.
An essential connection is with my heart   open and engaged
Creating not only a divergent idea   but adding unrefined sentiment
stirring the affect as well as the abstraction   shining an evocative light
on perspectives unforeseen   unenvisaged   unanticipated

I inaugurate that inquisitive place   circumstance   where mind and heart open
expand   allow fertile takes   expression   ways to share
previously unavailable possibilities that touch the world with adept ears
a blank slated mind where entrances introduce themselves and one honors
what shows up when the guardrails   for just a heartbeat   are removed
and life's breathe emerges in unfamiliar and refreshing form.

Creativity is seeing what others see and thinking what no one else ever thought.

— **Albert Einstein**

A question to consider with your writing:

If you fashioned a rebellious poem, prose, or prosetry, what might you write about?

4th Episode
Short Stories and Found Prosetry

You use a glass mirror to see your face.
You use the works of art to see your soul.

— **George Bernard Shaw**

A question to consider during this episode:

What is something you can't pass by without touching or smelling it? Write about that object/person/thing and the irresistibility.

Childhood
By Marianne Lyon and Geoffrey K. Leigh

The river of my childhood that tumbled down a passage of rocks came here and there to the swirl of a pool, and I see myself clearly as I knelt and then I see myself as if carried away, as the river moved on. Where have I been   where am I going? I was a bookworm back then. Collected hordes of volumes   lives of the saints   storybooks   hardbacks   softbacks. Mom was my Opus   my guide   by which I do not mean she escorted me to school   piloted me from ruckus play ground to library checkout housing stacks of authors I worshiped nor walked me to girl scouts   multiple badges awaiting. Once home   ahh   freedom in my special corner   my eyes swept over beloved pages   but one day she grabbed a treasured tome and threw it across the room. It bumped   slid open under the table   thump. I shout now for joy. For it was my time   my invitation to live.

But how? I lived from life jumping out of the pages   through textual adventures of playgrounds and stunning forests   waterways and boats   caves with magic lighting. I also play with my toys and listen intently   over and over and   irritably for my mother   over again to Peter and The Wolf. And   of course   my interactions with Charlie   who would fashion a play. What does he say about life beyond the safe volume covers? How do I move forth? Use your voice   he whispers. Gather grateful stories. Rescue a fold song. Sing those stories through notes and melodies. Ditty a rhyme. Harmonize great tales. Share your creations through jingles and compositions that others also may be touched in their hearts and stimulate their imaginations. But Dad was the music man   the whistler   the maker of life through tunes and songs   the player who could produce magic from that music box. Could I sing along? Could I become a music maker? The carrier of a tune with my vocal box? I begin to try. To share with him   without him   with anyone who might want to join in the vocal adventures and harmonic tales. As I progress   my throat comes to life with song as my carrier.

Then this morning I was gifted a miracle-time when a soft hand taps our front door. When I open it she warmly stares at me. I welcome her as I welcome my face in bathroom mirror each dawn. We offer each other a timid smile. I say   come in   a cup of tea? I slowly begin to feel that she is the myself I have let become a stranger. Closer   she says   let me whisper about a remembrance   a promise we made when we sang together under Grandpa's Apple Tree   bounced on Dad's knee   when we crooned loudly crossed our hearts to always remain inseparable. And I don't know how   but we rise and begin to hum   sing about the choosing of a ripened orb offering itself from low drooping branch. I hear melodic giggling as sticky juice runs down our chin. It happens so fast I barely understand when I give her my hand   as if it holds that precious fruit   but it really holds the cross-my-heart promise   the same promise we made under Gramps apple tree.

Trust in your intuitive self   that soft internal whisper that inspires the harmony of growth and life   let the vocal dancing express such inspiration to all around you   especially the children   teaching them to vocalize their hopes   dreams   joys   pains   while connected to their own whispers and sources of wisdom deep inside. Show them how to inhale the joy and exhale the challenges   all the time accessing the subtle information that avails itself to each of us when we pay close attention to its source of insight and discernment. And never silence the muse. Dad demonstrated the health of such approach   even during the difficult and weary times. And Mom exhibited such strength and determination   even with the blood drenched clothing that hung by the washer. Yes live   but not just exist   shine and sing your life   xactly as the breeze created melodies in the creaking branches of Gramps apple tree. For those who have ears let them listen to the sounds of life all around us. Query everything. Zen each day. Kiss each moment. Listen and breathe the song of life and love that comes though us when we allow.

Childhood: An Abecedarian Poem
By Marianne Lyon

A: Allow
B: Breathe songs of
C: Childhood
D: Ditty a Rhyme
E: Exhale challenges
F: Fashion a play
G: Gather grateful stories
H: Harmonize tales
I: Inhale their joy
J: Jingle all around
K: Kiss
L: Love the love that comes through us
M: Magic abounds
N: Never silence the muse
O: Opus a tune
P: Produce magic from your vocal box
Q: Query everything
R: Rescue a folk song
S: Shine and sing your life
T: Trust in your intuitive self
U: Use you vocal chords
V: Vocalize adventures
W: Whistle
X: Xactly like Dad
Y: Yes   live   not just exist
Z: Zen each day

The Writer
By Geoffrey K. Leigh

The novel begins to write itself as its author sits at his computer. New ideas and sequential events flow rather effortlessly, including enticing dialogue. He struggled earlier with conversations between his protagonist and a former lover. Creative interactions often required days to figure out where to go next. In this moment, ideas appear just as he finishes a previous scene.

Sergio relaxes as his fingers tap the black keys, forming new scenarios on his screen. The words appear from out of nowhere. He doesn't question it. He continues typing, hoping this emergent inspiration lasts until, at minimum, the completion of this chapter. The source remains an unquestioned mystery, for analysis of anything may remove him from the inspiration.

Was it this morning's strong black coffee? My dream the other night? he wonders to himself.

Stop, his internal voice yells. *Don't even begin. Just keep tapping.*

He does. Then he doesn't. Already, such ridiculous questions begin to distance his creativity. He stares at the keys for inspiration.

Anything. Just type anything.

His novel focus returns.

Antonio, Sergio's protagonist, spots a beautiful young lady in the coffee shop, sitting against the wall at a table for two with an empty chair. He so wants to meet her, to get a name, at least. A full name. And a number? Maybe that's pushing too far for this reticent young man.

The long straight dark hair falls down around her squared off shoulders, now hiding part of her exquisite face as she turns the book's page. She glances up as a man approaches and asks if he can sit there. She tells him no, she is waiting for someone, a friend, he thinks he hears her say.

A friend? A boyfriend? Possibly a girlfriend. Antonio wonders, but he'll wait and see.

Sergio continues to write, wanting to know himself what happens.

The attendant at the bar calls out, "Elena."

The young woman turns over her book and graces herself to the bar. Her full face smile thanks the barista. She returns to her seat and sips her coffee, then flips her book back over.

Antonio digs deep, searching for strength to stand, just for a moment, then makes the final decision to walk over to the table and say hello to this fine olive skinned model sitting alone.

Sergio glances at his watch, as it tickles the left wrist, informing him of the need to leave if he is going to be on time meeting Carlos at the corner coffee shop.

He now regrets having made the appointment. He removes himself from his chair, unfastens and sets down his sacred writing pendant, grabs his notebook, phone and wallet, then exits his apartment.

The street continues its mid-morning quiet, having delivered people to work and not yet busy with shoppers or the lunch crowd. As he approaches, Sergio opens the coffee shop door, allowing an older couple to depart, coffees in hand, before he enters. He scans the room, but no sign of his friend. He spots a young man at an open counter and walks over to order his usual black coffee, grateful he brought his notebook to jot down any new ideas that appear as he waits. The tables are less than half full, and he claims one on the far side of the room, away from the ordering line.

He glances towards the front door as he takes a trial sip of his black beverage, steam rising before his eyes, then scours the room.

His shoulders jerk as he straightens his back when he spots a young woman sitting alone at the far side of the room. Her olive skin and long dark hair create an uneasiness and intrigue. The hair falls from behind her ear as she turns a page. A man requests to share her table. She tells him she is saving it for a friend, who will join her. He leaves and she returns to her book.

A barista calls out "Elena" as she puts the cup on the bar.

The young woman turns her book over as she rises, retrieves her cup and sits again at her table, turning back to her read as she takes a sip of the beverage.

Sergio's eyes remain frozen on the woman. He wants to go talk with her, explain what just happened, with an attempt to understand the uncanny similarity to his typed words. But Carlos steps through the door, waves at Sergio, then gets in line to request his own drink.

As his friend sits down, Sergio begins.

"You won't believe what just happened," he says. "I was writing a scene in my novel that just played out when I got here."

"What do you mean?" asks Carlos. "Something happened here that was similar to what you just wrote?"

"No. What I previously wrote happened here just like I had described it. I think I might be psychic, as my grandmother once suggested," responds Sergio. "I think maybe I can predict the future."

"Oh, come on, man. No one really does that."

"Well, how would you explain what just happened?"

"How about coincidence?" laughs Carlos.

"This is too eerie and exact to be just a coincidence."

"Yeah, yeah. I think all this writing is getting to you, *mi amigo*. Maybe you should take it easy for a few days and avoid writing any more."

"I can't quit now. The ideas are flowing too effortlessly. I really like where this story is going. Besides, I promised my agent that I would have a draft to her in two weeks. And I need the money."

Sergio asks Carlos how things are going, refocusing on their customary conversations about life, politics, and Carlos's crazy family.

As Elena stands and moves towards the door, Sergio's heart sinks, as this opportunity to talk with her evaporates.

Carlos continues with his description of his maniacal mother's current illness and constant calls for family assistance. Sergio listens intently as possible, given his intense desire to return to his novel. After what he experienced as an eternity, he tells his friend he must get to a doctor's appointment, the only excuse he could craft to disengage himself from the current interaction.

Once back at his computer, he realizes how his protagonist can meet Elena. He begins to construct Antonio bumping into this appealing woman at the grocery store.

No, that's too pedestrian. How about a bar? No, a cliche. What would be unusual and interesting?

Sergio begins typing again.

He sends Antonio to the Department of Motor Vehicles to renew his car registration. In the curved line, three people ahead of him, stands Elena. He's certain. She holds papers in her hand, extending out of the same silky green and white blouse, denim jeans, simple blue flats as before, her shiny hair now pulled back into a pony tail, emphasizing her rounded face and ruby lips. Under the papers is the same book she had at the table, *The Catalyst Coalition*, a book he recently finished.

He watches as she moves to the next open window, hands the woman her papers, engages in a brief conversation, takes a slip of paper and moves to the waiting area.

Antonio looks around at potential open windows, attempting to estimate how long until he can get a number and wait. Typically, he abhors loitering. Today, waiting can't occur soon enough. Finally, a woman waves him over, he tells her what he wants, and she gives him a number. He immediately walks over to the only remaining open seat, beside Elena.

As he sits, he turns and asks, "How are you enjoying the book?"

They continue in a brief conversation that includes him seeing her at the coffee shop. Then a computer calls out Elena's number. As she stands, about to leave, he takes the risk of one question.

"Say, could we meet for coffee sometime to talk about the book? I'd like to get your impression of it."

"How about Friday morning at nine? Same place as this morning?"

Antonio's heart speeds up, his breath shallow.

"Sounds great. Thanks. See you then."

Elena goes to the window, takes care of her business and exits the building.

Sergio quits typing. He leans back in his chair and wonders about conducting an experiment. He used the DMV for the meeting place because his own registration page lay at the top of the paper pile on his desk. Now, he decides to test whether this morning's meeting was a coincidence or something else. He picks up the page, grabs his wallet and keys, and locks his apartment, them walks towards his car.

As he drives towards the DMV, he begins to wonder if he has lost his mind.

Why would I even entertain this? I'll feel like an idiot when she's not there. I won't even consider sharing this with Carlos, especially after ridiculing me this morning!

After he parks and gets to the front door, he stops for a moment, hesitant to enter. He suddenly wants to avoid making a fool of himself, even pondering this chance meeting. Yet, he must know.

He opens the door, steps inside and moves to the line with about five people ahead of him. As he looks around, there is no sign of Elena.

OK, I'm officially crazy. But at least I'll get my registration completed on time.

Sergio stares at the floor, lets out a deep breath, and relaxes his chest.

The man two people ahead of him shifts his weight to the right, revealing a pair of blue flats just ahead, previously hidden behind his large figure. Sergio raises his eyes slowly across the jeans, up to the green and white blouse and long dark hair pulled back into a pony tail, revealing Elena's captivating face.

She moves up to the next open window, gets her number and takes a seat. Sergio looks over to see a man and a woman sitting on each side of her. A small deviation, but close enough for his experiment.

The woman at the window waves him forward, inquires about what he needs, and offers him a numbered ticket. As Sergio grabs it and turns, he notices the woman sitting next to Elena left. He attempts a slow walk as he approaches the chair and sits, his heart pounding even harder. He turns to endeavor speaking with a calm voice.

"How are you enjoying the book?" he asks.

They chat for a moment, he asks about coffee as she stands, and she gives the same response he wrote an hour ago.

Sergio's body morphs from elation to confusion. He stares at the empty chair in front of him. When his number is called, he goes to the appropriate window, completes his registration, and returns to his car for the drive home.

What is going on? Am I making this happen? Creating reality? I truly don't understand this.

Writing becomes impossible the remainder of that day and the next. Sergio perseverates on his chance meeting with Elena at DMV. As he considers their possible interaction the next morning, he becomes abundantly clear he will not share any information about her connection to his latest novel.

Later that afternoon, he decides he will create one final test. He'll write down his sense of the conversation between himself, or rather Antonio, and Elena as they meet for their first planned interaction tomorrow.

How will she respond? What should I create? Or am I simply channeling Elena's life? Is she somehow informing me what to write?

Sergio begins to tap on the keys, describing a candid and decidedly intimate conversation between Elena and Antonio as they engage in their first prearranged discussion.

The interaction excites and gratifies Antonio, generating a desire for more. He asks if they might meet for dinner the next evening. Elena apologizes for being unavailable that night, as she is going to the movies with a girlfriend. She suggests they meet on Sunday.

The light beams through Sergio's bedroom shades early Friday morning. His anticipation of meeting Elena generated restless sleep and early awakening. He arises to shave, shower, then try several sets of clothes before deciding on jeans, a light blue polo shirt, and sockless black loafers.

He arrives at 8:45, wanting to claim the ideal table. There it sits, in the corner, with a man sipping his coffee. No book or paper. Sergio will purchase coffee and hover nearby with no other tables available.

Elena enters right at nine. The man at Sergio's table gets up to leave. Sergio pounces on it. As Elena approaches, he stands and asks what she would like. She describes her preferred latte, just as Sergio had written the previous afternoon. After returning, the two begin a conversation that stimulates similar feelings Antonio had experienced and continues for some time. Finally, Sergio asks about dinner tomorrow evening. Elena explains she can't, but would love to get together on Sunday. She is about to leave when he asks if she has another moment.

"I'm hesitant to share what I've been experiencing. But I can hide it no longer. You may think I'm a complete idiot or crazy. But I need to tell you something."

Sergio explains about his novel and how he described the first scene in the coffee shop almost word for word as it happened that day. He goes on to tell about the DMV encounter, how the same thing occurred between his writing and their personal interaction. Then he tells her about this morning, even describing the outfit Elena wears without having any clue what her wardrobe contained. Eventually, he runs out of words, a rare occurrence in his life.

Sergio looks into Elena's eyes, holds his breath, and waits for a response.

Elena takes her time before speaking.

"You are not an idiot or crazy. You are coming into your own energetic sophistication, as I thought you would. That's why I have been responsive to your invitations."

Elena again stops, looks deeper into Sergio's eyes for several moments before she continues.

"This is the reality of co-creation. It happens as people become increasingly sensitive to actualizing their own life while creating a deep connection with another. First, we tune into possibilities, starting with our dreams or altered states of awareness. We move towards anticipation of what most likely will occur with increasing accuracy, connecting to another's choice. It is never a given. But you become increasingly accurate with the co-creation process that involves an aware and active participant."

Sergio gradually brings his lips back together, wrestling with what Elena shared.

"Giving yourself over to writing allows you to see the possible without analyzing or judging the process," Elena continues. "Now, maybe you can do it without having to rely on the creation of fiction."

He puts his hand atop Elena's and allows the air he has been holding to escape. This part he didn't imagine in his story.

"Maybe," he says. "I do want to try."

The Writer: A Poem*
By Marianne Lyon

A novel begins to write itself
Breath shallows
Coincidence
Dreams
Enticing dialogue
First   turn to possibilities
Greet uncertainty
Heart speeds up
Inspiration
Just type anything
Keep typing
Lost mind
Making this happen
Never a given
Officially crazy
Psychic
Questions distance creativity
Runs out of words
Street continues mid-morning quiet
Truly don't understand
Unquestioned mystery
Very intriguing
Words appear from nowhere
Xenagogue guides the writing
You won't believe what just happened
Zoetic pulse abides

*An Abecedarian poem inspired by *The Writer* by Geoffrey Leigh

Coincidental Psychic?
By Geoffrey K. Leigh and Marianne Lyon

Inspiration   an unquestioned mystery   Words appear from out of nowhere   a novel begins to write itself   enticing dialogue   Ridiculous questions begin to distance his creativity for inspiration   *just type anything*   Young woman   full face smile   graces herself to the bar   final decision   say hello to exquisite face   Watch tickles left wrist   regrets having made the appointment   street continues mid-morning quiet   scans coffee shop for friend   He spots young woman alone   far side of the room   olive skin creates uneasiness and intrigue   uncanny similarity to his typed words   Friend steps through the door   sits down   "You won't believe what just happened   I was writing a scene in my novel that just played out here   I think I might be psychic   maybe I can predict the future"   "Come on, man   no one really does that   how about coincidence"   "Too eerie and exact to be just a coincidence"   "Take a break"   "I can't   ideas are flowing too effortlessly"   She stands and moves towards the door   his heart sinks   missing the opportunity to talk   Feels his intense desire to return to his novel   back at his computer   he sends his protagonist to DMV   in the curved line   three people ahead   she stands   simple blue flats as before   under her papers is the same book at the cafe table   *The Catalyst Coalition*   he walks over to the remaining open seat beside her and asks   "How are you enjoying the book   meet for coffee   I would like your impression of it"   "Same place as this morning"   His heart speeds up   his breath shallow   He quits typing   he wonders about an experiment   was this morning's meeting a coincidence   has he lost his mind   he parks at DMV   hesitant to enter   he opens the door   steps inside   no sign of her   *I'm officially crazy   At least I'll get my registration completed*   Man ahead shifts weight blue flats previously hidden appear   he raises his eyes across jeans   blouse   long pony tail to captivating face   after receiving numbered ticket   attempts slow walk to sit next to her   heart pounding harder he endeavors a calm voice   "How are you enjoying the book"   She gives the same response he wrote an hour ago   He perseverates his chance meeting   *What's going on   Am I making this happen   Creating reality   I truly don't understand this.*

*Found prosetry inspired by *The Writer* by Geoffrey K. Leigh

A Simple Seismic Shift
By Geoffrey K. Leigh

The pages fall together as the worn covers approach each other. The musty, earthy scent permeates his nostrils, reminds of other well-aged books he has savored. Uncertain when the bound ends might have last been ajar. Certainly not in the past three decades.

The read provided useful insights into the inherent impediments of Jainism. Another approach. Another set of constraints intermixed with the intended liberation from the cycle of rebirth. Possible achievement of moksha, the all-knowing state, attracted him to this particular belief system. Several gravitations and once again significant detractions.

He lays the rough leather covered tome on the return cart. His note filled papers retreat to the worn leather satchel. He restores the cap to his trustee purple and gold Levenger fountain pen and carefully replaces it in the appropriate cowhide pocket. With bag draping from the purple UW sweat-shirted shoulder, he quietly exists the library.

The air remains cool on this late autumn morning. Blown red, yellow and orange leaves enter into the bags attached to sweepers hustling along the university's approximation of manicured lawns. A few former greeneries cling to the branches, waiting to descend another day. Shoes carrying passersby bustle along the sidewalks or remain still as people chatter in small groups. A laugh or hugging slap on the back break the calm, with dissonant voices filling the air.

His loafers squeak against the solid surface of Red Square, past the little statue of George Washington, and beyond the tapestry advertised Henry Art Gallery. The read still ravages his mind as he crosses 15th Avenue and along 41st Street, then right on University Way. The direct approach. No patience for a meander. Discouragement fills his chest from the old book, wanting to finally identify a religious or spiritual path that satisfies his soul and impassions his thesis writing.

An older man holds open the Cafe Solstice door for him to enter. He nods, chirps out a thank you. Then searches for her. With good fortune, she landed the old round wooden claw foot table. It kneels in the corner, awaiting the appropriate two attendees. Its back cradles her coffee cup. Her body occupies the tall wooden chair against the puce green wall. She saves the captain's chair near the old red brick blockade for him.

He makes his way to the counter, unsure about another coffee to increase his caffeine flight. Quickly he spots it. The perfect brew for this morning's read. A shot in the dark. He orders a large, providing his hands a placement task. His phone beeps. He notices her request. He adds an order of lemon muffin to dulcify their conversation. Once appearing on the counter, he deftly retrieves and transports them to his reserved table.

Her eyes, once again, appear bright and clear. She wears her favorite grey cowl neck sweater accompanying jeans and black boots. With her hair pulled back, he guesses she did not wash it this morning. Her soft skin shines even brighter, unconcealed by her long black hair.

He places the muffin by her cup, his coffee near his seat and takes the chair. The warm lemon scent wafts towards him and faintly softens his mood. For the moment, he looks at her while assessing where to begin.

"How goes your research?" she asks softly, an assist to his assessment.

"Ran into more deterrents with Jainism. Like so many other persuasions," he says with such disgust that it startles him. His confidence fades with each exploration. Discouragement replaces hope. Irritation substitutes his waning inspiration.

"I'm sorry," she responds. Her hand reaches out to touch his. "I know this thesis provides more than just a research topic for you. But maybe you could focus on getting this completed. Then continue your personal inquiry into what path would facilitate your more personal growth."

His hand pulls back, stomach sags. Such responses contrast to the support he sought. His chest now feels weighted down further.

"I'm not sure I can. The more I read, the less important the thesis becomes. My need to answer this inner search is much stronger than my desire for the degree."

"But maybe take one step at a time," she offers. Her hand breaks off a piece of muffin, providing it a more functional task.

"That's nearly impossible," he responds. "The personal search drives the thesis. It's difficult to write when my heart focuses elsewhere."

He suspires slowly. The darkness in his chest increases, dampening his enthusiasm. He knows she wants to help. He desires to avoid disagreement. Yet, the sense of discouragement dominates his outlook.

"Could you simply pick the best one so far and use that as your main focus?" she inquires. "At least that would keep you moving and complete your degree."

He hesitates a response, considers her proffer, which grates against his desired find. He seeks more enthusiasm and useful alternatives rather than discouraging suggestions.

"Some days, I'm not sure I intend to finish. I don't want to pursue ministerial positions. Few opportunities exist to teach comparative religions these days. Sometimes I think the degree provides the incentive to continue my forage."

"Then why spend money on tuition with conditions imposed by others? What type of work would you pursue without the degree?"

"That's my dilemma. I don't know. A part of me wants to begin all over. After years of study, no religion provides promise. Yet, I can't let go. It drives me to find out. Understand. Find peace in myself. Then, I guess, I would want to help others do the same."

"Lofty goals. Not much money in that."

His heart sinks. Even deeper into the cataclysmic void. Such responses add weights to the hefty burden he already transports daily.

"More practically, I would like to teach. Comparative religions, I think. Maybe music. At some small junior college. Somewhere peaceful. Nurturing. Thus, the master's degree. A way to get me there."

"I know you love music. And your great at both piano and sax. But would you really want to teach that?"

He looks at her as he scrutinizes internally. A light wave of purple peace rises from the void.

"That's where I feel most serene. Most creative."

"Then why not modulate to the music department? Why not pursue that love and investigate religions as a side interest?"

With both hands on her mug, her eyes reach into his. Motionless, she morphs into a photo of inquiry, waiting to be taken. The wall behind creates a halo above her head. Clear as the question. Resounding into his confusion.

"I desperately want an answer. This inquiry feels too central to become a side interest."

"But maybe a new approach to this search would provide a fresh viewpoint. A change in how you look at all this may facilitate a new light on the endeavor."

"I worry it would fall into such a low priority that it may just eat at me without providing any substantive alternatives to what I've already learned. I fear it may increase my irritation with no substantial resolution."

She shifts in her chair, takes another sip of coffee, and, for a moment, stares at the brick wall behind him. As she recasts her eyes onto him, her voice triggers a crescendo.

"When you write a song or compose music, what stimulates an innovative piece like the way you ended your last performance? That provided such a unique sound. How did that arise?"

He leans back into his chair, taking the question internally for a ponder. He investigates such a creative process at times. Still unsure how it manifests.

"I hear a new sound, an interesting phrase, or see something that just triggers some place inside. Then the music or lyrics begin to flow. I don't know quite how. And I can never predict when it will occur. It shows up. I try to run with it the moment it appears. I don't know from where."

"How is that similar to or different from the way you explore a new religion?"

Now he takes another sip, providing him a moment to consider her inquiry. He feels caught off guard. Not in the way that someone suddenly accuses you of something wrong. More in the way that he just flows with the process rather than mentally analyzing it. She simply presses him to consider the approach from a new point of view.

"I'm in a whole different space when I work on music. The process becomes more integrative of senses and thought assimilated with feelings. I move into an unlimited space of creativity that is unbound by rules and norms, except where I find the limits of my abilities. Yet, even then, I can push those boundaries. That doesn't seem possible with my study of religion. The parameters already exist. I guess I limit myself in the study of belief systems. I have no experience to push beyond already defined limitations as I do with music."

She takes another sip, giving her a moment to consider her next remarks. The cup lowers to the back of the claw footed table. Her body leans forward. As if to tell a secret, voiding the ability of others to eavesdrop.

"Why can't you push the boundaries of religions? Why can't you challenge the perspective? What stops you from creatively displacing the fundamental view and limitations of belief systems?"

"I'm not sure what you mean. I'm not following."

"Do you believe each of us has a spark of any god or supreme being? If there exists some great consciousness, could we have a glint of that sentience?"

"I do. It sure feels like it when I'm in an expansive, creative space. Like sensing words or music that appear to come from beyond my physical being."

His body experiences greater expansiveness, a bud opening to warm sunshine that invites the petals to unfurl and caress a new world. Kiss the light and add beauty to the environment.

"Then why not view religions from the self to others rather than everything coming from the outside in? Why can't that creative process, awareness, also be part of our sacred, spiritual world? Why can't that be divine, as well? Maybe our spiritual or religious path is the nourishing of that glint of divine consciousness. That essence or light at our core, as Rumi describes. Such pursuit can't be any more destructive that religions have been, often spreading judgments, superiority, separation, and hate."

Another sip provides another moment to ponder. An instance to carefully consider what his friend is advancing. Her suggestion emerges crystal clear and vague simultaneously.

"I have been so busy reading religious writers, oracles, and philosophers that I seem to have predicated the same assumptions from which they work. I bought their perspective, as they have been perpetuating on others for centuries. As you ask the question, I feel a bit foolish."

"I suggest you waste no time with such a response. We all have. Maybe now is a good opportunity, given the fix this world and we inhabitants have created, for a transmogrification."

He loves that word. She is the only one who ever uses it with him. It suddenly stimulates a great transition from deep within, a clearing of the mud or cloud cover that prevents him from a grander vision. He searches his inner environs. He notices a light go off in his head, then in his chest moving down to the abdominal domain.

The shift stimulates excitement. It inspires an immense, visionary metamorphose. A seismic shift, not just in his vision. It becomes realizable. Supremer possibilities. His brain lights in multiple locations at once. His body overwhelmed. His creativity alive. His heart full.

"Once again, you have offered much to consider. I have no idea what I will decide. Yet, you certainly have provided me with many options. Overwhelming opportunities in the moment, and all possible."

He takes the last gulp of coffee, allowing another moment of reflection. The chatter in the room builds as background harmony to his inner melody. Internally, clarity and integration increasingly manifest.

"Thank you for your observations and perspectives. I feel freer on my journey. And love the connection between musical creativity and spiritual growth. What an innovative way to interconnect two areas I intend to pursue. Seems like my conservative religious upbringing has placed some blinders I have been wearing so long I could not even notice. At the moment, my eyesight feels improved."

"Just be aware that well used blinders may fall back onto your vision. The more you work with them, I think the less you will want to wear them."

He reaches out and grasps both her hands. He suspires slowly as he quietly blows out his breath. The exhale blows away much of the bundled weight he constantly transports with every step.

"Can we meet again next week? I think it would be good to discuss how this is going. I feel exhausted and stuffed right now. And I want an update with you. How are you doing?"

She smiles, her teeth gleaming, her eyes at rest. Their eyes reside in connection and communication.

"Generally, my life is fine. I'm working on one issue. But not ready to process it. OK to begin there next week? Some prep time would serve me well."

"Sure," he says with a chuckle. "Didn't know you would start the flood waves with a simple question, did you?" he adds with a smile.

Blended Views
By Geoffrey K. Leigh

Red wine became a staple in Jeremy's life on the day he reached legal drinking age. His parents previously shared small amounts of the beverage while growing up, a common tradition in his Italian father's family and a few others in Napa Valley. Although named after his mother's father, of Welch and English descent, his father's family played a more significant influence in his appeal for several Italian and most of the Bordeaux varietals. With his dad's guidance, he began to distinguish between Nebbiolo, Sangiovese, and Montepulciano. Then he began distinguishing between three of the closer Bordeaux varietals, Cab, Cab Franc, and Merlot.

Throughout high school and into college, Jeremy took his studies seriously. He enjoyed the botany class and became intrigued with the psychology, business, and marketing courses. He struggled to obtain a B minus in high school chemistry, apparently from too much fun that year. When the motivated student scantly earned a C in chemistry his first year in college, his concern of becoming a winemaker suddenly skyrocketed. He continued to learn about vineyards and the many aspects of management. He also loved his literature courses and begin to specialize in short stories; how authors designed them, learning about impact, and the pleasure of a surprise ending. But his heart became heavy every time he thought about abandoning his dream of becoming a first class winegrower.

Jeremy returned home that summer for a visit. Despite the joy of being near the manicured vineyards of the valley and a irregular bit of salty sea air from the San Pablo Bay, the weight of his failure remained ever present. It continued to crush his spirit. His dad immediately noticed fewer smiles and lethargic behavior.

"A bad semester at school, son?" His father inquired. "Break up with a girl friend?"

He knew Jeremy had few dates after high school. But when you throw a hook into the lake, sometimes you can snag a trout cheek.

"It was fine. Chem didn't turn out that well. I studied a lot. I just don't seem to get it very easily."

"There are lots of other majors. Do you have a better idea of what you want to do in the future?"

"I still want to become a winegrower. Botany went well. But microbiology was almost as bad as chem. I'm not sure I have what it takes to master these physical science courses, especially O-chem. I feel rather discouraged right now."

"Hang in there, boy," his father replies. "You don't have to excel. You just need a good understanding and know how to divulge the magnificence of each vino. Much of that comes from experience."

Jeremy remained unconvinced, even a bit pessimistic. During his second and third years in the enology and viticulture program, he thrived working with the vines from bud break to pruning, when the rootstock lie dormant, preparing for the growing season. This becomes a prime time for this budding winegrower to assess his own future.

Towards the end of his third year, Jeremy initiated a long conversation with his father, who had spent the last 25 years in sales with a large winery. They discussed other options in the industry besides making wine. His father enjoyed his work and liked marketing and connecting to distributors, restaurant owners, and sommeliers. But unlike his gregarious dad, Jeremy thrived as an introvert. He fostered numerous doubts a similar path would prove successful for this young man, who experiences more ease with wine than people. Yet his achievement in business and marketing far outweighed his competence in the chemical sciences. For an internship class, he began to work in a tasting room at a local winery.

He approached his initial decision to experience such a position with apprehension. He enjoyed talking with people. But meeting strangers day after day may well deplete his energy and any excitement he felt for the opportunity. Still, he knew he needed to experience other aspects in the business.

In preparation for the internship, his professor suggested he learn stories about the winery and how the vintner developed the business. He also explored how decisions were made about which grapes would be grown and any unusual choices or experiences that occurred as the winery developed over the past 40 years of its existence.

The first few visits took twists and turns in questions during the tasting that surprised Jeremy. Inquiries about the wine making process, decisions of when to harvest, and the pruning or grafting of vines he could easily explain given his activities in the cellar and vineyard. He added intriguing stories about the vintner that captivated the guests, increasing his abilities to create connections to the wines and location. Over the four month internship, his excitement to share and inform guests increasingly replaced his anxiety. But what astonished him the most was the internal message that confirmed this path. His view of becoming a wine maker resided in his head, while the confirmation for this aspect of the wine industry appeared more in his body, particularly his heart.

The completion of his degree became easier, worrying less on high grades and more about the information he finds applicable to his new choice of careers. He spent more time on wine marketing ideas and developing employees skills and success, now having replaced additional physical science courses with business and literary classes. During his final quarter, he began seeking a very different type of employment, one that combined knowledge of winegrowing and wine marketing. But rather than focusing on national sales, he wanted to begin working with wine tasting guests.

Given his father's connections in the local industry, he found a starting position in a small, family owned boutique winery. Daniel, the vintner, welcomed him and introduced Jeremy to the staff, including Sabine, the bright, talented and geeky winemaker.

The initial interactions with Sabine proved to be useful, while Jeremy shared his own assisting experiences in wine making. He also clearly expressed his lack of desire for a such a position, although he was happy to contribute if ever she needed his support. The two increasingly focused on their separate responsibilities, with a formal "hello" and "how are you" as they would pass. Not much additional conversation developed, and certainly not from Sabine's initiative.

One beautiful autumn day, immediately following an earlier harvest, Jeremy inquired whether Sabine would mark two or three barrels from the previous vintage he could use with guests to taste developing wines. She stopped and stared at him for a long moment, then agreed. Daniel already had informed her of his support for the request, primarily because he found it useful when he, in the early years, performed the combined roles of owner, winemaker, and host of any guests. Such barrel tasting provided differences in young "green" wines and more finished vino to newer high end purchasers. Experiencing the developing wines also provided guests an aromatic link to the entire winemaking process.

Several weeks later, Jeremy completed a tasting with guests. He returned to the cleaning area and pulled the wine thief out of the first cleaning tub. Sabine noticed him allowing the water to drip back into the barrel before putting it into the second and third cleaning solutions.

"Don't put the cleaning water back into the container. It will leave possible wine residue and contaminate the solution."

"OK, if that's the way you do it here, I'm happy to follow your system," Jeremy responded.

"It's not just my system. That's the way you're supposed to clean things. If you don't know what you're doing, maybe you shouldn't do it," Sabine growled.

"It's not what we did at my previous winery. I didn't know you had a different method."

"Well, you should know. Or maybe just keep to your sales area and don't mess up the wine making process."

Jeremy could feel his heart sink and the heat permeate his face. He wanted to walk away. Just leave and compose himself, before he said something he would regret. He took another deep breath and slowly allowed the carbon dioxide to release.

"Are you actively involved in what goes on in the vineyard? Or is that a separate area in making wine?" inquires Jeremy.

"Don't be ridiculous! Of course it's an important part of the process. That's why I have winegrower on my business cards. That's been a deep connection since André emphasized the process decades ago." The smirk on Sabine's mouth widened as she finished her remark.

"Then if nurturing the vines and growing stressed fruit is a central connection to making bold, intense wine, why is nurturing committed purchasers and long time buyers a separate element to the process? Why do you emphasize the importance of the vineyard supervisor cooperating but spend no time in collaboration with the hosting supervisor?"

"Because you're just selling the wine. That's all you need to worry about. That's all you care about."

"Oh, is that so? Then why am I out in the vineyard pruning and harvesting? Why am I on the bottle line or paying attention to what the workers are doing with the fermentation and barreling? Given your split responsibilities with two other wineries, you don't see all that I do here and care about. And that's why I introduce you to our guests when you are here. So they have a more personal connection with the entire process of making great wine, which increases their interest in becoming long time purchasers and consumers of the high end vino you make. If I and others who do shipping and emails don't sell the wine, you wouldn't have the funds to keep making it."

Sabine stopped talking and simply stared at Jeremy's face. She appeared as a deer in bright headlights, not sure what just occurred.

"Well, of course it's important to sell the wine. But just focus on that. Beyond selling, it has little to do with the vineyard and wine making."

"Really? Do you think greater numbers of people come during harvest because they have no interest in the process? When they ask about pruning, grafting, how the harvest is done, and what type of barrels we use they only care about the outcome? The attachments people make to the winery don't rely just on their tasting experience or whether they love the wine. They connect to the stories and the impassioned connections to the whole process and encounter. And while we can talk about it in the abstract, I'm increasingly certain that the sensual experiences with the wine, people, and process produce the deepest attachments to the winery and its vino."

Following another extended stare, Sabine responds. "I have things to do. I can't waste my time with you trying justify your mistakes."

With that, she traipsed into the wine cave to continue her work.

For several days, the two employees walked around each other in an innovative avoidance dance. While Jeremy noticed the tension in his stomach, he also paid attention to the ease in his heart for the emotional clarity with which he spoke to Sabine.

Following a week and a half of the uneasy dance, Sabine came up to Jeremy and asked if they could talk. He breathed deeply and replied that he had some time.

"OK. I see what you mean about the connections between our areas. I think I wanted to simplify my involvement so that I needn't worry about anything else. It was easier to simplify my responsibilities, given my pressure from other locations. But you're right. They all are connected. And I'll take some time to walk you through the way I like to have things done. Then, if we need to discuss changes or compromises, we can do that."

"Thanks, Sabine. I would very much appreciate that. I'm willing to incorporate your process when and wherever possible. I know the importance of making sure things are clean and don't introduce problems into the winemaking process. I just want to help people connect deeply into what we do and have a strong emotional as well as intellectual connection to us and the wines. I want guests to experience a deep link between the development of intense flavored hillside fruit as it transforms from vineyard to barrel to bottle to consumption."

"I've never thought about quite that way. But I agree with what you're doing and the importance of such connections. How about we meet set up a time early next week, when you don't have guests, to walk through some protocols. Then, if you have any questions or possible changes, we can walk through them."

"That sounds great. I'll check my schedule and text you a few options. Then we can explore how we can support each other rather than separate connected systems."

"Ok. I'll see you next week."

Sabine shared a bigger smile than Jeremy has seen since he arrived at the winery. This facilitated a deep breath and slow release on his part. While his developing connections remained somewhat of a concept, the discussion had pushed him to transform it into a tangible reality.

Finally. Maybe we can begin to be collaborators rather than combatants, he thought.

Suggested writing prompt:

Write about somewhere or time in your life where you moved from separation to collaboration.

The Alterant*
By Geoffrey K. Leigh

The apartment windows invite luminescent beams to bounce off the warm cream walls, embracing all who wander through, from the sitting space to her generous sleeping area. Even the bathroom frequently finagles toasty rays into the far shadows of the shower.

This roomy nest became her abode over nine years ago, when the old mattress warehouse first transformed into loft apartments. The high ceilings and open space provide a sanctuary from which to explore the city, walk to work at the gallery, make new friends, and allow space for venturing into a Promethean style of painting. Fortunately, the new construction overwhelmed the smell of the former manufacturing.

This morning, she mounts the new, ornate full-length mirror procured yesterday at the antique store. She cherishes the wooden figures that frame the old fashioned glass, particularly the doves swallowing angry creatures emerging out of flames. The crafted consumptions sooth her heart and generate internal peace, despite the violent underpinnings. Scent of the old frame elicits reflections of helping her father with his wood carving hobby. The double braces on each side will secure the hefty mirror for years of pleasure.

She steps back to admire her creative efforts. The symmetrical armature encases the frame, focusing the whole wall onto the ornate mirror. Satisfaction affirms the intuition to place this framed reflection in such a prominent location to the right of her easel. From that position, light ricochets from the outside glass to innovative locations in the surrounding space.

This will do, she affirms. *Yes, this will do well here, I think.*

Once she assists tools to relocate into the bag and take their place along the back wall of her studio space, the blank canvas, framed just prior to her antique adventure, places itself evenly on the worn easel. A fresh receptacle, encapsulating many possibilities. But what provokes her most today remains the burgeoning of inner turmoil that has been mushrooming the past few months.

The canvas gets primed with oil to prevent leaching, followed by a solid macabre backdrop for the remaining choices. She methodically selects colors of pigment sticks that will portray the murky churning she experiences against its inner dingy ambience. She loves the softer consistency of oil sticks and the hint of linseed. The tray nominates midnight blue for initial circular contours from nowhere to nowhere. They simply exist. Yet, the overlay begins to characterize her interior atmosphere.

Forest green becomes the subsequent nominee, sometimes overlapping the blue. More often, it provides its own grim contrast and form. Next, eggplant purple adds more depth, some contrast, and an alternative turmoil for the circular disarray. Finally, a blood red adds its own fuel to the molten cumulation, with counter circular elements disrupting any vacant expanse. The scent of the fresh paint and oil provides meager relaxation of her abdomen, even if temporary.

As the design focus appears, her interior atmosphere punches into full bloom. The image on canvas begins to clearly depict her convulsive experience.

She returns the brush to the palette, drapes small chaotic orange onto the edges, followed by scarlet, highlighting the blaze that seethes randomly around the periphery. With few bright colors beyond a small measure of orange and red at the edges, the somber pigments overwhelm the landscape. These final highlights evoke images of the irritation and tenderness most noticeable when sentient of the mucky gloom.

A few steps back allows her to grasp her new composition. Rather than comfort arising from the recreation, nausea ensues. She steps back further and collapses into her appraisal chair. Her latest formulation provides accuracy and revulsion at the same time. Her head turns away, unable to concentrate on her creation.

What is wrong with me? Why all this darkness and gloom? The counseling seemed to help for a while. But now I'm feeling even more lost. More depressed. The muck is infectious.

In a desperate attempt to morph her sentiments, she moves to the mirror.

Maybe a few positive affirmations will help once again. Can't hurt to try.

As she sits in front of the mirror, her body falls forward. Suddenly, she is on the other side of the glass in a whole different environment. Everything appears amorphous. Her father is present and telling her how ridiculous she sounds when sharing her desire to become an artist.

You'll never make a living at that sort of thing, her father tells her. *You're not that good, you know. Give it up. Do something productive, like I do with my printing business. You might get good enough to design if you work a lot harder at it. That would pay. You could live on that.*

His mouth moves, but the sound comes as much directly through the brain as the ears. He points his finger at her in the same manner he did when adamant about his opinion. The firmest aspect of her current state targets the volcano erupting in her abdomen. The episode reminds of a recent dream she experienced and hastily disappeared into a fog. Her current interaction feels more like her life, including the inability to rapidly escape.

The strangest contrast to her initial dream is that she had the sense of embodying a young girl. Now, in this dream, she remains her adult self. Yet, the sentiment feels formative, youthful, when her father would share such dictates. He remains present. The decrees grow dormant.

She scrutinizes her environs. Little appears available to assist an alternative response. She pays attention to her glacial anatomy. The only accessible warmth is the inner volcano on the verge of eruption. Yet, her desire remains devoid of destruction. Her mouth opens and the lava flow transmutes into solid words escaping from the oral fissure.

I am not you, Dad. I can't live life your way.

The comments erupt heavy and hot. The fire refrigerates as the molten expression exposes itself to the atmosphere. The comments contain less sting while remaining firm in their denotation. The pungent aroma of smoke dries her throat. The eruption begins to subside while the molten altercation endures.

For me, innovation for others' ideas doesn't sooth like fresh originality from within. I may not become a great success. But avoiding such an imaginative venture produces inner execution. To paint is to live, thrive, flourish, even if no one else agrees or values my efforts.

She hesitates, then perseveres.

Is it possible that such a decision in your own life drives such reactions to mine?

No overt response occurs from her father. Her internal reaction did not require one.

Abruptly, she falls back through the mirror. At first, she remains unsure whether she initially fell into a dream state or into one coming back through the glass. She pinches herself. While she feels slight pain, she remains unsure.

The volcano recoils, the molten flow recedes. She ploddingly stands and saunters back to her inner portrayal on canvas.

The likeness to her previous state remains. Her present abdominal condition reflects her ease and assuagement following her interaction with Dad.

The focus shifts to a contrast between her current interior circumstance and the painting. What previously appeared as simultaneous ordeal now reveals an opposing distinction.

Having transformed her interior state, she can see the beauty in her creation. The depiction stands strong, powerful. Relief erupts, permeating her body. Instead of representing her internal turmoil, the beauty of the curves, deep colors, and contrasts stand out as an elapsed disturbance, eloquently represented. An inner state transformed.

After some time savoring her new piece, she carefully takes the canvas to her drying cupboard. The second recently framed canvas takes its place on the easel, where she primes it with oil. Then she takes a spot of lunch.

In the afternoon, she paints a sky blue background except for a long, vertical white rectangle in the center. When dry, she begins creating over the next few days an even more inviting brown frame for the mirror, with trees and bushes surrounding the casing and a few nebulous ones in the white center, as if in a dreamy mirror environment. Next to the distinct tree outside the brown frame, she paints the backside of a woman standing, looking into the mirror at an angle. A seated women's face reflects back to the erect figure. In the distance off to the right of the perched female stands an amorphous male, not reflected beyond the frame.

The second painting depicts, to her at least, the mirror adventure that endures in her memory, a bit illusive yet invincible. Unsure such an adventure could reoccur, a memento could prove invaluable.

Over the next few months, when not on duty at the gallery, she continues her work at the easel. Her images produce less exuberance than her two previous compositions.

Her time sitting in front of the mirror proves useful for her affirmations. But it fails to entice a similar shift through the glass.

As she studies her latest painting from her appraisal chair, her thoughts drift to an old Norman Rockwell illustration, a copy of which hung in her mother's kitchen. The picture included a husband and wife having breakfast together, yet each in their own world. The suited man reads the paper with hat and briefcase at his feet. The well-dressed woman holds a dainty cup of coffee, gazing off to her left with flat affect. No interaction at the tiny table. No apparent connection between the couple.

She decides to create a painting of her own parents' breakfast relationship. She finishes it within the week, with two cups of coffee at the table. A crumpled newspaper rests by one cup. A lost woman stares at the empty chair, her mug held with both hands, scruffy hair, dressed in a frayed bathrobe. The women's face reveals a disoriented gaze. She can almost pick up the steamy aroma of her mother's coffee.

As she examines the finished product from her chair, she revisits her own sense of lost. While studying her mother's face, she realizes she at least partially internalized her mother's primary attribute.

Yet, how could I not take some aspect of that? After all, I modeled her in some positive ways. I don't put up with angry men. But I also want to recover from such separation.

Once again, she strolls to the mirror and sits in front of it. She examines her eyes to see if there is some hint of her mother's attribute in her own face. As she looks, she falls into the mirror's interior dreamy atmosphere.

Her mother is there, crying as she did when her father finally left to be with another woman. She dreamt this scene many times as a teenager, frustrated with the dream on each occasion.

Why couldn't you find the strength to move beyond Dad's leaving? she asks her mother.

Her mother stares back at her. No words escape her.

I love you, Mom. And I don't want to hold on to that part of you. I want to free myself and embrace my strength, even if I never marry. I know you tried. I must do more.

Even in this amorphous setting, her life begins to experience greater reality than on the other side of the mirror's glass. She suddenly realizes increased uncertainty as to which side is a dream and which is reality, if such opposing states exist. Now, each side has a fundamental difference, one no more real than the other. Except that all her paints remain on the other side of the glass. Still, she has come to enjoy this place, where all her symbolic and rapturous existence provides an opportunity for resolutions that commonly continue in a static existence on the other side.

As she falls back through to the other side of the glass, her sense of lost is replaced with a sense of missing. A part of her continues to exist on the other side of the glass, possibly never to be completely united with her strong, artistic, purposeful self. Still, she appreciates the contrast and ability to experience the difference. She seeks to unify the unequivocal clarity she experienced on the far side of the mirror with the robust, intentional self of this side.

Now, one more image calls to be created. She frames one more canvas and primes it. On paper, she creates the basics of a scene she wants to paint.

Again, a mirror shows up. This time, it is a plain wooded frame dressing mirror. She stands slightly to the side gazing into the mirror. She wears her painting clothes. Her face depicts a strong, confident woman, medium cut hair with one side pulled behind her ear. She has a slight, inviting smile and bright eyes.

The figure in the glass depicts a lost, scared to be alone female wearing a nightgown, slippers, with uncombed hair. Her lips are drown down and eyes vacant of life.

The two sides of her. The options she faces, from her younger self, drawing on her mother's fears. Or the woman she wants to be, with an open heart for the lost part of herself. Which part will prevail?

She realizes the strength found in the interactions on the dreamy part of the mirror could be her salvation. But only if she remembers and continues to choose on the side with all the paints.

*Inspired by and dedicated to Ellie Leigh.

Missing Parts
By Geoffrey K. Leigh

The repair estimate paralyzed me. I knew some replacements may be needed over time. This prognosis demanded a sizable investment for which I was not ready. While the attendant suggested a few items could be delayed, I held a paper indicating nearly $7,500 worth of improvements to keep my reliable 2003 Honda CRV running. Yet, the worth of the vehicle, from what I could gather Online, remained about $2,000 on a good day. While it had been a while since I checked, I doubted the value had increased much. Even with the surge in prices for used cars during COVID, my high mileage vehicle seemed an outlier to the increases. The ability to avoid a new car payment and to continue use of a reliable vehicle provided much greater value than that to me.

In addition to the car's age, the vehicle already traveled over 248,000 miles. Yet I knew the previous owner and I both created a history of excellent care. I hoped to achieve a 400,000 mile outcome, a new record for any of my cars. It felt like a worthwhile objective given the junk already produced by our consuming society.

I had started a part-time job at a winery. A full-time hilarious host remained popular and guests requested him frequently. His long-time friend worked a couple of Saturdays a month. I remained unsure how many hours would fall my way, especially during the late autumn and winter when visitors notably decreased.

I loved my involvement in such a setting. A dream come true for me, even with doubts in my qualifications for such a position. Their wine became will respected. And every one of their estate wines I consumed teased my palate with pleasure. The oakiness of the barrel room along with the aging of wine instructed my nose and lifted my spirits. Visits to the sacred room made sales easy for guests who fell in love with the place as I did.

The news that the regular winery host would become a father and take time off put me in a more favorable temporary position. I continued to learn more facts about wine varietals, process of pruning vines and tying the canes, useful details to share with guests. I also felt more comfortable telling stories about the owners, how his parents acquired the land and he started clearing and planting the vineyard while a young man. The work remained enjoyable and stimulated my interest in the history and process of winemaking. These circumstances increased my comfort with the income as a winery host. Still, the position was seasonal and steady income remained uncertain.

A ray of hope for some reduction in the overall expenses came from my insurance coverage for a new windshield. That reduced the repair estimates from $7,500 to $6,400. I also purchased a couple of replacement parts at a discount through a local store. In addition, the service advisor recommended looking into quality parts made by other manufactures that might lower repair costs. That possibility appealed to me. But I needed to think through the total commitment before he began the investigation of alternatives.

I took several days analyzing my options before making the decision to repair the old car. I called Dan, the dealer repair advisor, and asked him to begin an inquiry regarding non-Honda parts where appropriate that might lower my bill. He told me I would hear from him by 10:00 am the next morning. Given a busy time at the winery and my volunteer work at a local community organization, I had plenty on my plate to keep me busy. I heard nothing from Dan for two and a half weeks.

Following the delay, I called and left a message with Dan. But I never heard back from him for another two weeks. I knew the repairs needed to be done. With everything else going on in my family, including interactions with my four children as well as their families and the CRV running well, immediate repairs were not my highest priority.

The following Monday, I took my car in for a new battery, as the old one became unreliable. I could not forgo transportation to my job. Dan was not there that day, so I talked to another service representative about possible alternative parts. She agreed some items would remain high quality and decrease my bill. She would leave a note for Dan to remind him to contact me.

I continued to focus on winery work with the inclusion of more stories about the owner and his family. I also began to collect humorous sayings and jokes that might increase the guests enjoyment while tasting wine. My confidence continued to increase, with major doubts pushed to the sidelines.

As time passed, I experienced relief with the decision to make a significant repair investment rather then commit to years of car payments. With my home now paid off and sufficient social security to cover some essential items, the commitment to keep my Honda going felt like the best compromise. My part-time seasonal position heightened such a resolution and easing my financial requirements would allow me to breathe more easily.

A friend who lived in San Francisco suggested we spend a day off visiting art galleries in the city. It sounded like a great idea, especially since I avoided going there for some time. Rather than drive and deal with city parking, I decided to leave my vehicle at the Vallejo Ferry garage and sail over. Michael said he would pick me up and take us around. It sounded like a lovely day, especially with a radiating sun that day.

I arrived for what I thought provided perfect timing to get onto the ferry, purchase a cup of coffee and enjoy the ride. I misread the schedule and was very early for the next one. A cafe at the terminal provided a spot to savor some better coffee with a bite to eat while looking at the homes with a view and the ship yard across the inlet.

When the ferry arrived, I found a spot early in line and claimed a seat in the upper deck to enjoy the ride across the bay. Travelers were chatting, laughing, working on computers, or attempting to continue their morning recovery with an additional snooze. Having finished my beverage, I walked around for a while, then used the rest room just before landing.

With busy morning traffic, Michael arrived a short time after I departed the city ferry terminal. He pulled into a loading area and I climbed in. We chatted as we headed for the Museum of the African Diaspora. When we arrived, we found it was closed that day. Instead, we drove to a museum I had not visited located in the well know Lincoln Park.

The Legion of Honor escaped my awareness over the years of visiting the city. We decided that would be a good place to start, with a casual lunch to begin our exploration. The Legion Café Ruben melted in Michael's mouth, while the Norwegian Smoked Salmon Galette aroused my palette. The outdoor seats increased our relaxation and gratitude for the setting.

We first enjoyed the Tudor exhibit, which proved fascinating and educational. Finally, we toured the Rodin sculptures. They stunned and astonished me. As we left, we experienced the external Holocaust exhibit, a gut churning yet simple portrayal of the deadly conditions, dampening my uplifted spirits from the previous exhibits.

We began the drive back to the ferry, stopping along the way at Michael's favorite Cambodian restaurant for dinner. He then dropped me off at the terminal, just in time to walk onto the ship. The entire day became filled with beauty and appreciation for art work, delectable refreshment, and easy conversation. A spontaneous experience that inundated my body and heart.

The return ride allowed for reflection of a relaxing and idyllic day. I felt ready to return home as I walked off the ferry and into the parking garage to retrieve my vehicle. I reminisced my stroll through the Rodin gallery, the magnificence of his creations, and the vision he perceived in the raw materials, removing all that detracted from his final perception.

My car appeared sound in the dimly lit garage and the darkness beyond. I looked forward to getting home. When I turned on the engine, it sounded like my quiet CRV transformed into a hot rod.

Unfamiliar with many automobile details, I remained uncertain how to determine or conclude the cause of such a dramatic change, though a couple of possibilities came to mind. I suspected what had happened while I continued to go through many possibilities. I felt semi-confused and shocked, embarrassed, both for the noise and my lack of expertise to verify the cause.

Then the anger arose. The invasion and assault on my poor automobile. Anger turned to rage, in part for the helplessness that swallowed me, unaware of how to remove myself from this bombardment of clatter.

Given the lateness of the hour, I decided to drive directly home. I wanted more than anything to get out of this I pulled off on the side of the rode in American Canyon and confirmed my suspicion that a significant piece of the tail pipe had been removed from the underside of my CRV. With no shop open that late into the evening, I continued the journey home. Luckily, no police stopped me for polluting the air and noise environment.

Early the next morning, I took the chance of driving my newly created hot rod over to the local dealer. Dan was there and helped me get it in to be inspected. A few hours later, my suspicion was confirmed. The catalytic converter had been removed from my car, which also left the vehicle without a functioning muffler to quiet the exhaust. In fact, my car had been immediately converted to a hot rod. The cost of the repair? An estimated $5,500, on top of the other repairs still needed.

I become distraught. I couldn't afford another repair. And in its current state, my vehicle contained no value, except possibly for a few parts.

Dan suggested my insurance might cover the repairs. I immediately called my agent. Yes, in fact my insurance covered a missing catalytic converter. I called the number to talk to the department about repairs. The agent told me he would get back to me as soon as he discovered the value of my car.

A short time later, I received a call from the claims agent. He informed me that my car's projected worth lingered slightly more than the estimated repairs. The difference remained so little, especially with the other required improvements, that the insurance company would have to declare my car totaled. On the other hand, he shared some good news. He estimated the car's value at about $5,800. With my $500 deductible, I would get around $5,300. They could pick up the CRV from the dealer and take it away that afternoon or the next day.

I took the remainder of the day to figure out what to do. I felt discouraged about losing my paid off reliable vehicle. I had no idea what to purchase as a replacement. And I doubted my ability to obtain a suitable loan for a relatively new car.

A friend picked me up at the dealership and took me to my daughter's place, where I could temporarily borrow her vehicle She and her husband drove his car out of town and wouldn't return for two days.

I got home and began immediately to do a search for a good used vehicle. I needed to figure out what available options existed in my area and how much I could afford to spend. I called my credit union, where I established a pretty good history, even with a small credit rating problem. A clerk told me about an auto services division of their credit union just an hour away from my home. I looked at the website and found a two year old Toyota Prius Prime that could be driven by battery and/or the gas engine, with low milage.

I wanted to get into electric vehicles, but I couldn't afford to upgrade my home to a higher charging station that most vehicles required. This car could be charged from a regular home outlet over a longer period of time. I had an outside outlet and plenty of time overnight to charge it. This appeared to be a great compromise.

In case I agreed to have my care totaled on paper, I went back to the dealer to empty out personal items from my vehicle. I had driven the CRV for 13 years and felt an attachment. I didn't give it a name as some do. Still, it felt like family, having delivered me to many places, including transporting all my gear to Burning Man for several years. While cleaning out the back, playa dust remained under the back rug and in the wheel well. Between the oil and lubricants in the dealer service area, evocative of an early gas station job, and the scent of playa dust, it became an hour of reminiscing my life adventures.

I called the claims agent the next day. I told him to total my CRV and send me the money. He could transfer it into my bank account within a few hours once the car had been removed from the dealer. I also emailed the auto service division, informing them of my interest in the car. I drove to work, hosted some guests, then left immediately after to see the potential new car.

When I saw the clean, two-year old silver Prius with black interior, my interest increased dramatically. The redesign of the vehicle that year made it look much sportier than previous models, and it appeared in very good condition. When I drove it both in the city and on the freeway, it had good pickup and a comfortable interior. My interest continued to surge.

When I returned the car, I talked with an agent about what I needed to do to purchase it. I had looked around at similar models in the area, all of which were $2,000 higher or more. Given that the dealership was connected to my credit union, it became easy to apply for a loan. She also could see the available funds for a downpayment. When she told me I would qualify for a loan at a little higher interest rate because of my credit problem, I told her I would take it. I then went back home in my daughter's car to figure out how to get a ride back the next day to pick up the car.

Within 24 hours, my CRV was gone, the funds had been transferred, and the Prius became my new vehicle. Not before signing my life away, off course, with a new loan. But I saw no other option. In the end, I began to figure out how to use as much of the battery power as possible and enjoyed driving a newer vehicle. Given my limited options, I became comfortable with my new loan and ways I might pay it off early. And the heated seats, which I had only enjoyed in other people's cars, later would caress me on cold mornings for the challenge I had faced in this entire transition.

Several days later, I reflected on the whole process. I suddenly realized that the anger I had focused on Dan for not returning my earlier calls and getting things lined up to have my repairs completed altered into a blessing. If he had been quicker at finding auto parts, I may have invested over $6,000 in repairs and then had my car totaled from the stolen catalytic converter. Suddenly, I felt gratitude for the delay.

Sometimes I felt like the universe conspired against me. This time, I felt blessed for the timing of the events.

Good living? I doubted it. Lucky? Absolutely. Gratitude? In full!

*Don't be satisfied with stories, how things have gone with others.
Unfold your own myth.*

— **Rumi**

Transitioner Accomplice
By Geoffrey K. Leigh

The old woman, nearing death, lies motionless on cushiony bedstead. Her tangled hair protrudes in random directions. The bodily covering, dry and scaly, attempts to retain heat with succor from additional blankets to thwart the chills from a recent snowstorm.

Family tears hover near her, desperate to prevent, hold for dear life. Helpless. Desirous. Wanting. So full of grief for something not yet complete.

In the corner, I observe the mourning dance. Well known, all too familiar. The inner drive to grasp the graspless. My energy focuses on Margaret as she wavers at that gossamer-like threshold separating this world and the vastness beyond. Her eyes focus on my astral presence.

It's OK, I telepath a whisper to the old woman. *I am here to support. I'll travel with you into the next venue and remain until you find your comfort bearings. There is no need, at this juncture, to hang on to this locale. When ready, let go. We'll journey together for a short while.*

But I'm scared, Margaret responds. *I'm terrified of becoming lost, evaporating, nothing. Or worse yet, going to Hell!*

Be at peace, my dear. I've helped multiple times, Relax. All will be well.

The room becomes humid from tears. A daughter holds mother's hand. A son wipes her brow. Others now share their love for Margaret. Mother. Grandmother. Cherished teacher. Angry neighbor. Loving friend. Rigid disciplinarian. Avid gardener. Devout Catholic. Terrified patient.

The old woman responds to daughter's squeeze. Slowly opening eyes, she looks at those gathered. Weak smile appears on withered face. Desire hovers, as Margaret seeks to care for those who surround her.

Energy and ability ebbs. Her body weakens.

Any attempted comfort of others becomes too great for this diminished patient. Fragile smile remains her sole recourse.

Just breathe. Slow, deep breaths. And relax. These can be important moments in the transition. Savor them and your current connections. Yet, mind the attachments.

I'm afraid, Margaret responds mentally to my suggestions as she closes her eyes. Her lime green nightgown lowers as she exhales. *I don't want to disappear into nothingness. Or face my judgment.*

My dear, I suspect your inner judge has been overly active much of your life. Let her rest. There is no forthcoming judgment greater than yours.

How do you know?

Well, OK, I don't know all. But that has become my observation with many assists of this transition. It seems for most people, they are their own harshest critic. Even when it's buried beneath their narcissism. That's just another defense.

But I don't want to face God or anyone who will judge me. I'm exhausted from these final months of suffering.

Just rest, Margaret. All will be well. Trust me on this one. Be with your family during this loving goodbye. There is no rush.

Once again, she opens her eyes. A tear escapes down her cheek as I send energy to her heart, with hope for expansion.

Her midsection contracts as another sharp stab creates an increase of agony. Margaret rolls onto her left side toward her son, a hand pulls out of daughter's grasp. Her essence separates from her body, floats near the ceiling.

She looks at me and smiles as she removes herself from painful anatomy.

Is this how you began to leave your body? Margaret asks.

Yes. During the pain of my cancer recovery. My thoughts attempt to serene the scene.

Is your body in pain now? Is that how you escape it?,

No. My body rests in my bed and is fine. I have learned how to depart at will when someone can use assistance.

And how do you know when people begin dying? Do you spy on them?

I smile at Margaret, my astral body approaches her at the ceiling, looking down at the moist family gathering.

A family member contacts me. They hear about my assistance and want help with relatives or friends who seem especially afraid of death.

How much do you charge for this? Is this how you live, profiting off people's sorrows?

I accept only a thank you. It remains a gift I offer when I have a sense that my presence might be helpful. I meet with the family or friend, request an understanding of the dying person, then decide if my succor seems appropriate. Or at times, I feel summoned when someone, nearing death, cries out in emotional agony. I may feel their cry and respond to the trembling clamor.

Margaret looks back down at her imminent corpse and her family circle. Suddenly, her essence retreats to her body. Her physical eyes open as she recovers her original position.

She takes her daughters hand and presents it to her canoodled lips. Then she does the same for her son. Her expiration of breath prompts an anatomical emancipation.

I guess I'm ready, Margaret shares, the fear residing predominantly in the corpse.

Take my hand. We'll travel as slowly as you desire.

We ascend beyond the home roof, moving upward at a steady tempo. Margaret feels more relaxed while continuing to clench some anxiety.

Do you know where you're going? Margaret asks.

I hold a sense as we leave, and we are usually found. It's like someone follows our bearings, so I don't require a specific place in mind, I tell her.

Could I find it without you? inquires the old woman.

Yes, or greeters converge on you. It's not so much the destination that is important as not becoming engrossed with attachments to people, events, or places from your life that don't allow you to disengage. That's more my purpose than guiding you to a a specific place. And helping hold a calm atmosphere.

Ahead, we view several astral beings, as if waiting for our arrival.

Welcome, Margaret, telepaths the woman in the center of the gathering.

Margaret smiles at them.

Dear mother, it's been a long time. Dad, Jeremy. It's so good to see you all again.

I hold back as they engage. Then Margaret's mother turns to me.

Thank you, Jamal. We'll take it from here.

Her eyes glow as she looks into mine.

May the reunion be savored and joyous, I share.

I turn and head back to my place, to reunite with my physical form.

It was fortunate that this transition occurred during the night when my body could rest. I arise at 7:00 am and prepare myself for work.

As a man approaching middle age with no partner, the lack of need to explain my restless sleep some nights or what makes me want to share this gift eases my life. It is five years since my breakup, and the flexibility in my routine and commitments relaxes me.

The next evening, I tune into my subsequent transitioner, Tony. He feels close to the shift. Less anxious than Margaret. Anger permeates his body. Time feels close. No need to attend in the moment.

I maintain input of any change while I continue to write the following day. My sense remains that transition will occur in the next 24-48 hours.

As I sit at my desk, confusion ensues as to how to end my novel. Part of me wants to create a touching and joyous ending by my protagonist marrying the woman with whom he has felt the most intense connection in his life. The flip side, emerging from my depressive past, focuses on the protagonist's death, possibly tragedizing an ending that could stimulate a desirable screenplay.

In order to release my quagmire, I begin to outline how each ending might proceed. Still providing no solution this afternoon, I go to the kitchen and pour a glass of reminiscent Zinfandel.

After my second sip, I feel the pull to visit Tony. I retire to my bedroom, lie on the soft bedcovers, then withdraw my astral being and expeditiously enter Tony's bedroom. His son, Lorenzo, sits by his father's home hospital bed. His daughter, Emma, on the other side, lays a cold compress on her father's forehead.

The room is gloomy, with only a small lamp on the table next to Emma. Light from the hallway illuminates Lorenzo's back more than his face. Having spent time talking with Tony about his fear of hell, I know his sad eyes and droopy smile. The room shares scents of fresh yellow roses and mentholatum.

I notice movement on the far side of the room. Another astral body appears near the ceiling in the corner over Emma. After a brief moment, she looks directly at me.

What are you doing here? she asks.

My face suddenly feels like one large question mark.

Lorenzo asked me to assist his father because of his immense fear of hell, I tell her. *Who are you, and why do you appear now?*

Emma asked me to assist her father. She thought a female would be helpful because of his deep sadness for Sophia, after their divorce several years ago. Emma thought her dad might not want to move on.

A sibling conflict, apparently. I dislike getting in the middle of those. Lorenzo assured me none existed. Guess he was not as clear about that as he thought.

She asks, What name do you go by in this incarnation?

Jamal, I respond. And you?

I'm Chiara. Nice to meet you, even in the middle of a conflict, she tells me.

I'm not sure how to resolve this.

Well, she says, I can help with his fear of hell and his attachment to Sophia. I suggest you allow me to help him with this transition.

I guess you're right. I'll be leaving then. Best with the process. I trust all will be well. And maybe we'll meet another time.

Yes, that would be nice, she says.

I make a courtesy wave as I leave the room, feeling like Tony is in good hands. And I doubt Lorenzo will ever know, unless he follows up, as some do, to ask how it all went.

Back in my bedroom, I remain curious about this chance meeting. I'd heard of other transitioner allies, but until today had never met one. And particularly under such stressful circumstances. She did seem pleasant.

I return my body to the desk, with a feeble attempt at additional writing. My concentration difficulty increases with my curiosity about Chiara, how she began, the frequency of her assists, and what else she does with her life.

Finally, my questions recede as I amplify my concentration on writing. My inclination lies with the death of my protagonist as I begin to script the process of his demise. Clarity of my decision increases as I proceed to write, although my heart does not concur. I tend to find cheerful conclusions more satisfying, possibly enhancing hope for my future. Yet, I continue down this path of extinction, particularly as my marriage dissolution reemerges.

With no other clients to assist, I can focus on my writing for extended periods of time. I think of Tony from time to time, wondering if all went well. I assume so. And I heard nothing from his son. Then my attention turns back to my work, determined to create an ending that includes both death and wonder of what else might have happened.

In the late afternoon the next day, I hear a knock on my door. I open it, restimulating a question mark face.

"Chiara! How did you find me?" I ask.

"Do you have a little time? I'd like to update you on the process with Tony, for your own sense of completion."

"Yes. Of course. Come in," I tell her. "Have a seat anywhere you'd like. Could I get you something to drink?"

"Some water would be great, thanks."

She sits on the far end of the tan, well-used couch. After getting water for us both, I sit in the worn brown chair facing her.

"Thank you. I just wanted to let you know that things went well with Tony, after some discussion of the futility of hanging on to Sophia. I think her daughter was correct. And I want to thank you for making the shift so easy."

"I'm glad the transition went well. Happy your intuition was correct. I'm only interested in what's good for the transitioner. It's not about me."

"I agree. But I was so surprised to see you there. I wasn't sure just what to do. You made the shift effortless. I appreciate that. "

"That's my intention. May I ask how you got into doing this assistance?"

"Sure." Chiara suspires slowly. "It began about two years ago, when my daughter got lost in the Sierra National Forest while hiking with a friend. Rescue workers looked for several days and couldn't find them. She's my only child, and her father passed away a few years before. I panicked."

"I don't blame you. I think I would, too," I respond.

"I was so stressed one evening, I simply exited my body. I was shocked at first, not understanding what happened." Chiara takes another deep breath, allowing the air to escape slowly.

"It's an amazing feeling when it first happens, isn't it?"

"Oh, yes. Then I decided to focus on my daughter's energy, flying over the forest, to hone in on her. I finally found her and her friend. I couldn't help them directly. But I figured out how to identify where they were. The next day, called the officer who had been updating their search progress. I told him where to find the girls. They did, later that day, to my great relief."

"Didn't he ask how you knew?"

"Of course. I told him I had a very vivid dream. That seemed to satisfy his curiosity at the time. And we've talked a few times since then."

"I'm so glad they were alright. Have you done it with others since then?"

"Well, yes. Last night. I wanted to meet you and let you know how the transition went with Tony."

Chiara pauses and looks into my eyes.

"And I wanted to know another ally in this process. I've never met any others before we connected in Tony's bedroom."

"I haven't either, and I'm glad to know you. It's nice to know another. But how do you do this? How did you find me?" As I say this, I wonder again how strange my face must look with this inquiry.

"People seem to leave an energetic trail where they've been. It fades eventually, kind of like your scent that bloodhounds follow. But I went back to Tony's house, picked it up again, and followed it here. I hope you don't mind," Chiara responds as she cocks her head to one side.

"Not at all. I'm happy to see you. I kind of have a sense of how you do that. I guess, its a bit like we lead the dying person to a meeting place, even though we don't know the exact location. But I'd never thought about it in those terms. I'll pay more attention to it, now that you've described it."

"Well, I won't keep you. And I have errands to run. But very nice to meet you physically."

"Great to meet you, as well.

Would you like to go to dinner sometime? I telepath with great hope, too anxious to ask verbally. I don't want my ears to hear a no.

Yes, that would be nice.

I notice a tightness in my chest that begins to ease.

How about this Friday?

Yes, that works for me.

She pulls out a card from her green blouse pocket and extends towards me.

Here's my number and address.

Great. I'll pick you up about 6:00?

Perfect. I'll see you then.

We stand and walk to the front door. I open it and she smiles as she steps outside.

"I'll see you Friday," she says as she walks away.

I watch her go.

I return to my desk and sit for a while, contemplating my recent experience. I turn towards my computer and decide to rewrite my novel ending.

Insightful Clusters
By Geoffrey K. Leigh

How

How can imagination expand to inspire, envision, create, share
Allowing one to paint, express, mold, dance like no one else

How might brain, eyes, hands, heart expand to possibilities
Others could not allow themselves to unfold

As she reads the words of her latest poem, Lucia walks through the vineyards for the last time. The thoughts she penned in an old notebook resonate throughout her body, as she seeks insight to the nearly unanswerable questions.

She wants to create previously unimagined wine that expresses her creativity and incorporates her drive to make each a vintage outstanding. She realizes, as a young winemaker, there exists choice to poetically write her life. Simply getting out of her own way becomes the challenge.

When her father becomes gravely ill, just three years into her first assistant winemaker position, her mother insists Lucia come back to manage the family business. Although work at the larger establishment remains interesting and an opportunity to expand her skills, she prioritizes her loyalty to the family's Oenophilia Winery. She remains grateful to be working with Lorenzo, her father's experienced and talented winemaker, with whom she grew up crafting elegant *vino*. The transition into this new position offers greater ability to impact the outcomes and a broader array of experiences. But the price she pays means less support from a variety of perspectives .

Her only sibling, Marco, commutes between home and college to assist the family with Angelo's care. He focuses on completing his advanced music degree and demonstrates little interest in growing or making wine. He provides no insight or support to her process.

Her ability to craft great wine emerges ostensibly from her whole being; blood, palate, brain, ancestry, and energetics. Yet, like great fashion, Lucia realizes she also must frequently reinvent this fine beverage through the assemblage of varietals that work together effortlessly. At the same time, the accumulation must appeal to people through the nose, mouth, and magic connections made with others when they visit to taste the wines. Can she do all this? Does her commitment compensate for her lack of experience and diverse levels of support?

The transition to her family enterprise came immediately. She gave notice with the blessing of the current winery administration. This is her final walk through the harvested vines she will not see through fermentation. She plops on the ground at the end of a carefully crafted Cab Franc row of vines, to continue the review of her writings. Lucia notices the stiffness of her body and the ascending scent of fall in the air.

> How can one manifest creation that becomes unique, magnificent
> When no previous being could caress the canvas or play on paper
> Fly across the floor, construct with clay or stone
> Such visions escaped those before them, now lost in the multiverse

Lucia returns to the winery, then loads her final box of personal items into her worn upholstered truck and drives home. She realizes the transition will not come easily. Yet, she feels some sense of reverence returning to her small family vineyard.

She continues to listen and learn from Lorenzo. The study of her craft becomes increasingly important. She pays attention to every detail. She desires to know more, try new approaches and see what works best. Each vintage will become another opportunity to express her creative passion, to create wine that enflames a person's nose, mouth, heart, and soul.

As she settles into the new position as proprietor, an emotional charge amplifies her connection to this place. She desires each vintage to express the *terrior*, as the French label it. Additional responsibilities include interactions with guests, as Angelo created strong personal bonds over so many years.

Lucia begins to talk with people as they come to taste Oenophilia wines. Conversations oft include life plans and ambitions of their guests. The lack of career passion and excitement expressed by a significant number of visitors puzzles Lucia.

After long days in the vineyards and winery, Lucia assists her mother, who focuses all her efforts on Angelo's care and comfort. Giulia focuses much of her time on her husbands increasing inability to relieve his pain.

Her father's frequent low groans from the liver cancer encourages Lucia to explore information about medical cannabis. As they experiment with different flavors of indica, she notices Angelo's ability to relax longer and exhibit fewer bouts of restless allows him to turn towards peace.

Eight months after the discovery of Angelo's aggressive cancer, he passes away. Although ten years Giulia's senior, everyone who knew his high energy and happy smile experiences shock with the rapid decline in Angelo's health.

For Lucia, a part of her working body has been removed. Something that provided support to stand tall, encouragement to explore, desire to improve has been eliminated from her life. Yet, she knows her mother depends on a daughter willing to trudge forward, keep the work progressing that generates the family income. She now will need to incorporate her own source of strength and maintain the determination that has brought her thus far.

Following the celebration of Angelo's life and visiting with family, Lucia returns to her room. Doubt, for the first time, seeps into her abilities. Her clarity of purpose turns cloudy. She again pulls out her recent writing, created when the inner sun warmed and illuminated her creative endeavors.

> How does the magical creative expression emerge
> Open to places and sources beyond one letter, step, stroke at a time
> Hands in clay or pen on parchment while head reaches for clouds
> And heart expands beyond the chest, touching something galvanic

She may have known her vocational path when she emerged from Giulia's womb. Lucia remembers wanting nothing else. When she played with dolls, they were working the vineyard, managing the canopy, or cleaning the tanks. Her tea set served imaginary wine in it, either white or red. But it always comprised the fermented beverage, even when Giulia gave her water for the cups. While her descriptions remained simplistic, her clarity persisted.

She grew in her father's vineyard, where she learned wine growing lessons and insights from his decades of experience. Lucia asked incessant questions when she didn't understand, pressing Angelo for answers to satisfy an overly curious mind. Giulia at times became irritated when Lucia would mess up her spice cupboard, attempting to name different spices and scents while blindfolded.

Even the little details became important. She pressed to know how professionals held clippers when harvesting and what needs to be removed when sorting grapes before first crush. Her agile body allowed easy access to clean the fermentation tanks. Her obsessive streak created beautifully painted barrel bilges using the wine lees to identify aging red wines, which cover spills when topping off barrels or drippings from the wine thief to assess maturational wine progress.

As Lucia developed, so did her agricultural skills. By age eight, she could keep pace with most of her father's vineyard staff. She surpassed her brother's pruning, even with Marco's two years additional experience. But such competition remained less challenging, as he would rather read or play the piano. The dedicated vineyard manager, Roberto, would share his secrets and show her tips for improvement. She would practice on the newly planted citrus or fig trees, *espaliered* at the front of their house. None of those trees ever looked less manicured than the vines that produced their family income.

By the time she entered high school, Lucia became obsessively attached to Lorenzo when not in class. She grew adept at punch downs to keep frequent contact between skins and juice in bins or pump overs with the large tanks. She tested the fermentation process while wanting to home in on the smell to decide when the juice should enter the oak barrels. Once in the barrels, Lucia would clean and sanitize all the equipment. Here, her obsessive-compulsive side would morph from irritation to asset, much to Lorenzo's gratification.

In her senior year, advanced placement chemistry and biology became top priorities for this aspiring enology student. Once she completed her reading and assignments, Lucia would read books on botany, geology or the history of wine making. She became fascinated by the art of blending wines, adding a creative streak to her scientific interests. This synthesis of left and right brain hemispheres intrigued her.

Her parents encouraged her pursuit of wine growing and making. Angelo especially appreciated her assistance, though the deluge of questions at times became prodigious.

Giulia, a writer and poet, never wanted to hinder Lucia's pursuits. Yet, mother also encouraged her daughter to arouse some other artistic ventures in her life, such as creative writing, ceramics, or music. At the time, little else interested her daughter.

Her mother shared poetry when Lucia first began to write words. She revered the way her ingenious parent would integrate ordinary words to express stunning events, scenery, and internal struggles with reverent and penetrating descriptions. She loved creative alliteration and the way words could evoke strong emotions and descriptive scenes by the creative adjoining of different phrases, senses, and imagery.

She first read Robert Louis Stevenson's famous quote, "Wine is bottled poetry," after her wine growing initiation in her father's vineyards. In an instant, she coupled her two developing loves into an intertwined future. She became determined to render fermented beverages that enticed the nose, awakened the palate, and enhanced connections when shared among friends and family. Then she would attempt to describe such experiences in an unconventional and innovative fashion.

Lucia attended a local college so she could return on needed weekends, especially during harvest. She enjoyed her academe experiences and friends she made, particularly those pursuing an enology degree. In contrast, Lucia became flabbergasted with the number of friends and classmates who had difficulty deciding on a major and career, or when some seemed unexcited by their intended objectives. Such indecision and lack of motivation remained an enigma to this prescient student.

When she read Albert Camus in her philosophy class, Lucia became even more astonished when he described the life of someone doing the same routine as "absurd." He seemed to overlook or ignore the passion someone might have about their work, one's enthusiasm to create winemaking art out of science. Camus ignored heart excitement from one's work and adventure of inception for each vintage. She didn't understand him, and his work generated little interest in her. At the same time, she remained puzzled by his philosophical analysis and conclusions. The most positive aspect remained the development of hope in relation to work. Lucia instead focused not on a general hope, but on one's life passion.

Angelo suggested Lucia gain familiarity with procedures and processes of another vineyard and winery after graduation. She realized this would expand her repertoire of methods and possibly become exposed to other grape varietals. She agreed with her father's suggestion and became excited about new possibilities.

She took a job as an assistant winemaker at a nearby large winery that grew two Italian vines, Nebbiolo and Sangiovese, as well as all five Bordeaux varietals. They also made a Super Tuscan blend of Cabernet Sauvignon with Sangiovese. She began referring to this as a Fretalian wine. Maybe her mother's creative writing encouragement began to blossom.

When not working with or reading about wine, Lucia continued to write poetry and increasingly a combination with different forms of prose. Yet the creative expression lacked something. An element remained missing. The mental painting felt unfinished. The poem not complete. Even great wine did not completely fill the increasing void.

Feeling into the current pain of her father's death, Lucia feels unfinished with her work. She loves creating great wines. But a missing piece, the uncompleted poem fills her abdomen. She reads the last few lines of her recent work.

> May such magic permeate arts and science
> Forging new frontiers from a place once viewed ordinary
>
> May the muse touch head, hand and heart
> For creation to flow freely and manifest a world previously unforeseen

Lucia stands, changes her clothes, and decides to walk through the family vineyards. They frequently bring her peace. Today, she needs even more.

While she strolls through harvested rows separating the Sangiovese and Cab Franc vines, Lucia spots very different mushrooms growing off the trunks of both varietals. She plucks up a sample to take back to the house, wanting to identify whether they were edible or poisonous. They appear similar to either Caesar's or Bay Bolete mushrooms, yet not quite either.

She shows them to her mother, who loves to include mushrooms in many different recipes.

"I'm not sure what these are and too risky to take a chance. Why don't you take them to the Farmer's Market on Thursday and ask Michael, the mushroom guru, what they are," suggests Giulia.

Thursday morning, Lucia drives to the market. She wants to get some fresh produce for her *madre*, and her body bursts with curiosity to label the newly discovered vineyard mushrooms.

"Oh my," says Michael as he examines and smells the sprouted fungi. "I do believe these are Psilocybin 'shrooms."

"Do you think they are safe to use?" inquires Lucia.

"Oh yes, quite safe," Michael responds. "Safe, if you want to journey. They're not safe if you don't. But they're not poisonous, if that's your concern."

"Thanks. I appreciate your insight."

Lucia begins to worry about the wine already aging in barrels after an early fermentation. She returns home, leaves the fresh produce in the refrigerator, then she walks to the barrel room. She grabs a wine thief, glass and two sterile flasks along her way. She removes the bung from the barrel of Sangiovese, inserts the thief and sucks the developing beverage into the metal tube. She pours some into the flask, the remainder into the glass and takes a sip. She savors the wine, getting beyond the greenness of the flavor in an attempt to taste any rot or decay from the vine. Nothing shows up from the taste. But she knows a lab analysis must be completed to provide scientific confirmation. Then she repeats the process from a barrel of Cabernet Franc. The second tasting also provides no evidence on her palate.

The nervous proprietor goes to her office and calls the lab. A runner comes later that day to pick up the samples for a more thorough analysis.

After delivering the samples to the runner, she returns to the barrel room to taste another sample. Maybe she missed something in her initial assessment. Sensing a queasiness developing in her stomach after another sip, she decides the day has been intense and consuming.

Lucia walks to the house and goes up to her bedroom, grateful all the people have left. She sees her mother's closed door, and indication she, too, is resting. Her brain increasingly lights up, as if someone just increased the grey matter dimmer from low to medium. Her thoughts scramble at first, then zero in on her choice to lessen commitment to her life dream. It is all still there, right in front of her. The sadness at the loss of her father's steadiness and Lucia's clarity loosened her own sense of purpose. The choice to walk her path also stares at her, waiting for which she will choose: sadness or clarity. Then, the choice itself interweaves. There is no force pushing these two apart. They both are real and possible. They both are part of her. One does not dismiss the other. The separation occurs when she focuses on one and ignores the other.

The next day, she informs Lorenzo that she wants to blend the Cab Franc and Sangiovese into a 50-50 Fratalian wine. She thinks it will be a lovely vintage combination. She wants to call this wine their Awakening Blend. Her winemaker looks at her and nods.

Two days later, a lab official informs her they find no evidence of rot or decay in either sample. The tests were all negative, although they did find a hint of fungi that was distinct from the typical yeast in such wines. They wondered if we were using a unique yeast to help with the fermentation process.

The following day, Lucia hosted two guests from Seattle at their winey. They had a lovely conversation, including a discussion about spirituality and life purpose, for both were wearied from their jobs. One of the women asked Lucia if she were spiritually inclined.

"My spirituality is sharing great wine with caring, loving people. I attempt a daily practice by including consumption of the sacramental beverage for clarity and awakening. Come visit us again in two or three years, when our Awakening Blend will be bottled and ready for consumption."

Restorative Connections
By Geoffrey K. Leigh

Another failed relationship. Another heartbreak. Another onset of discouragement, tantamount to depression.

The petite two-bedroom apartment suddenly materialized into an immense space for his contracted body and broken heart. The white walls radiated sterility and the institutional carpet disseminated malaise. He went into his unlit closet, where he could see neither, to make one last desperate call. A final attempt to explore any chance they could mend this tattered connection.

Rather hostile and firm, Sara stonily informed Dylan, after a very brief request and discussion, essentially there was no chance in hell any mending would happen.

He hung up the phone with tears rolling down both cheeks. He thought she was the one. He became thoroughly convinced even before they became lovers. This was the greatest connection he ever experienced. But her magical relationship remained with her second husband. Or at least that became her response as this relationship began to sour. For Dylan, this connection evolved into his 'Juliet.'

Now, his dream mate's response approximated the announcement of Juliet's death. His lifelong search for his true love ended with a poisonous call. At the time, Dylan wished for his own death. What was the use of living?

And all this after considering suicide when he felt like he didn't have the strength to end his marriage many years ago. He knew his marital relationship became destructive for both partners. Hope allowed him to dream of a future Juliet love. For the first time in any relationship, he felt support for his ideas and contributions. Embraced the way he was. At least until acceptance swiftly dissolved. He could not imagine this perfect relationship would last only a couple of years and disintegrate after hurt feelings by one of her daughters.

With tears tapered off and dry on his cheeks, he emerged from his closet drained and in need of refreshment. He stumbled to the kitchenette for a glass of water, then retuned to his bedroom. Dylan took another sip of water, placed it on the bedside table and crawled into a ball on his bedspread. He felt the dried cries attempted serge. Yet, the tear ducts, like his body, ripened into debilitation.

Dylan slept for a while, but lethargy lingered upon awaking. He decided a couple of cannabis hits might make him feel better. While not used frequently, such medicinal therapy often helped bring him out of the depressive state and allow a broader view, an expanded perspective. Fortunately, he possessed a small amount for just such occasions.

He walked his weed filled pipe and lighter down stairs and out beyond the parking area where he could remain unnoticed and undetected. He took his first inhale and held it momentarily, then released the smoke from his lungs. As he perceived the onset, he took a second puff. After crushing the embers, he walked back upstairs to crawl onto his bed and relax.

His body began to soften. The depression began to dissipate bittily. He could breathe again, although he remained unsure he wanted to do so. He let his mind go blank, as he suspired slowly in and out. With eyes closed, he began to feel his body and energy. He paid attention to the sluggish expansion of both as he continued to breathe, the depressed state still providing some resistance against expansion. Wondering where this might lead, he noticed less pressure to cry and the darkness evolved into a gun mettle grey instead of stark black. His chest became lighter.

To his left, he sensed the energetics of a warm, caring woman. In the beginning, Dylan took the awareness as craved make-believe. With his only entrance locked, his rational mind knew no one could possibly appear in physical form. Yet, he felt some type of presence and thoughts coming into his head. He sensed movement, even sitting on the side of his bed, her hand touching his back, roughly at the location of his heart. The energetics presented compassion without intrusion, kindness without sympathy. Simply a loving presence.

He wanted to open his eyes to look, yet he didn't want to lose this connection. Still, his curiosity got the best of him. He turned, eyes open, only to confirm no woman in physical sight.

As he closed his eyes, his energetic sense remained clear. A presence, some unseen being, remained close. Dylan loved the sensation of her and wanted to remain connected. Given the unfamiliarity of such an occurrence, he remained lost as to how he could preserve it. After some time processing the question, he nodded off into a light sleep, his body exhausted.

Over the next few days, Dylan managed to see his clients and complete his therapeutic notes on previous sessions as the depression continued to dissipate. His focus moved away from the experience to things in his world he could control. He remained unsure whether to trust his senses or his local mind. Yet, there lingered something magical and essential from the energetic occurrence.

A week later, Dylan decided to see if he could reconnect with this energetic presence without the aid of cannabis to expand his senses. As he attempted to make himself as comfortable as possible in his lumpy bed, he telepathed an invitation for her to appear once again. He suddenly felt her presence by the side of his bed, with the same comfort and care he experienced during her first emanation.

This time, he decided to trust the visitation while also seeking some additional information.

What is your name? he asked mentally.

He felt unsure whether any response occurred. Then he heard it.

Fadima, she seemed to say.

His body trembled as he felt the response. He never considered any ability to communicate with this presence, this being, this female form, unable to be seen with his physical eyes. In his heart, it felt real, however.

Do you know me? Have we met before? Are you alive on this earth or a being from beyond?

Dylan worried he now overwhelmed her with an inquisition. He didn't know how to retract his requested information.

We knew each other in a past life, Fadima responds. *Presently, I utilize an energetic body. If you trust this process, I can assist you at times.*

Fadima's responses reassured him that he was not going crazy or about to die. Her presence apparently was not related to his imminent death. At the same time, he worried about losing his mind, going crazy. His heart suggested this whole interaction would be fine. But who can trust information from an unfamiliar organ.

Over the next few months, Dylan hoped he can meet someone who embodied Fadima's energetics and support of him. His desire ultimately focused on meeting Fadima in the flesh.

He assessed the energetics of each new woman he met. Even if she were married, they could become dear friends. He believed that would satisfy his soul. As a bisexual male, he wondered if her energy would show up in a man. Even with all these options, he couldn't seem to locate such a feeling he experienced with Fadima's energetic presence.

His hopeful search began to transition into discouragement. He wondered if even her presence no longer became an option. He decided another attempt to invoke her energetics might rectify his yearning.

That evening, upon retiring early to bed, he mentally called out for a visit from this being, still new in his life. He attempted to open his heart and again telepathed her requested presence. Again, it took only seconds for him to become aware of her nearness and support.

Are you not in physical form in this world? he inquired.

No, not at the moment, she replied. *It is easier to assist you in this form during this incarnation.*

But we have been physically together previously?

Oh yes, several times, actually. And in each case, we were emotionally and heartfully connected, no matter how we manifested or what form each of us took.

So why are you not in physical form this time? Why couldn't I meet you while you also had a body?

This time, I wanted to support your energetic development. That also seemed more important for sourcing your inner strength. If I show up in physical form, I engage in wonderful support for you and your work. But that does not exercise your energetic trust, either in yourself or our relationship. And I didn't want a physical relationship to distract you from your life's work.

But I'm unclear about my life's work. I feel so caught up in the physical and survival mode that I seldom focus on such a question.

Then it's time to make a shift. Time to learn more about who you are beyond the physical form. Time to begin trusting beyond your physical senses, Fadima shared. *Lack of support in the physical realm pushes you to continuously exercise the inner strength in order to stand tall and solid from the essence out rather than shrink and dissolve away.*

Dylan felt unsure how to respond. He had considered writing about some of the ideas he worked on over the past few years. Many focused on parenting with an open heart and healing early wounds that make people sensitive and reactive to stated or implied criticism. While he attempted to heal both issues within himself, he remained an aspiring student of the practices rather than a seasoned professional. Still, utilizing them in his therapeutic practice increased his deployment, even if not his confidence.

For the next several weeks, he would write in his spare time. He began with advice pieces for parents, one of which was picked up by a local magazine. With more experience, he embarked on fictional short stories to get his points across. In this way, he could share ideas through interesting characters to reach other audiences. He enjoyed the creation process and the lack of need to reference other researchers or theorists required in professional writings.

As he continued with his therapeutic work, elements began to creep into his responses with clients that included more focus on heart openings before couples engage in discussions or as part of date nights he frequently recommended. Expansion of early wound healing also increased in his therapeutic focus. His clients found it useful to reduce reactivity to his or her spouse's comments, which could also diminish their own anxiety and anger.

Yet, Dylan still would get triggered by a snide comment or off-handed remark. After one recent submission to a local anthology, a review included a remark about how common his ideas were and recommended the story not be included. Two days later, a client became upset at one of the therapeutic heart opening suggestions Dylan offered, saying it felt too 'hokey' to bother doing. The combination of such remarks this time wounded him deeply.

That evening, Dylan enjoyed a glass of Cabernet Franc with dinner, then sipped a second glass as he relaxed on his back balcony. Tears again felt close and discouragement began increasing like redroot pigweed in his small garden.

Before you can help others open their hearts, an essential ingredient becomes the opening of your own on a daily basis, shares Fadima.

Astonishment overcame Dylan. He had not requested her presence. But he felt comforted that she appeared anyway. He breathed into his heart and focused on it opening as he eased further into his chair. The cool evening breeze helped soften the organ as it relaxed and increased its energetic opening, a physical surrendering.

Thank you, he replied. *For coming and for your recommendation.*

Of course, she replied. *This is the role I chose and love sharing.*

Are you such a loving women when in a physical body, too? he inquired.

Dylan sensed she chuckled at his interrogative.

Of course, I have tried, Fadima replied. *Being physical makes it more challenging with all the competing issues, senses, and demands on a corporeal life. That is where choice and priority become so important when manifesting in a body. It's still possible. But it takes clarity and strength to carry that out over time.*

And are you always in female form when you support people here, he asks.

On no. I could be male, too. Or a combination of the two. I chose female because women have been most supportive in your earth life. I thought I could reach you more easily and you would experience greater trust because of growing up with important female support. But I could show up male next time, if you like. Gender is more fluid than people view it in most cases.

You mean you can just change genders, as you desire?

Again, Dylan has a sense of laughter from Fadima.

Humans get so caught up in categories and dichotomies, especially around concepts like gender. When in fact there is all sorts of evidence that even in physical bodies gender is not just one or the other. Babies are born sometimes with elements of both genitals. Even doctors are confused at times. And not all women or men show up the same. There is so much variety of manifestation by the way women and men manifest their gender. And for bisexual people, like yourself, you manifest parts of both genders, even with one type of genitalia. Allow yourself to be less rigid. Less judgmental of others and what they are like. What the physical gender tells one and what the emotional or identifying gender expresses itself is not always the same. And does it hurt anyone, except those who are closed off to other possibilities? It's the categorization that hurts the most, not the manifestation.

Dylan began to anatomize her last comment. He knew a lot of the research to which she referred. And her perspective confirmed what he had been considering for some time. Her clarity felt refreshing, actually, even if the sharing of that might not feel comfortable to clients. Still, some stilted categories like this needed to be challenged. And he would incorporate such ideas into his writings.

While her comment felt comforting, his weed patch became noticeable once again. The criticism of him continued to discolor his view of himself and his therapeutic and written contributions.

Yes, Fadima commented. *There still remains the hurtful comments, both verbal and written. We can talk about where we agree. That contains the momentary distraction for the deep wound you experience from other people's responses to your work.*

Do you spy on me or watch me? How do you know about those things? Dylan asks.

Oh, no. I do not spy. I don't need to do that. I simply pay attention to what is in your heart and the wounds in your body. It's the same wound we tried to heal in our last incarnation together. But you would not tackle the issue fully. You did not remove the root and allowed the wound to remain and spread into this life. That is why I wanted to attempt this type of connection for your current incarnation. Maybe I could help you more this way than being in physical form. You could more easily dismiss what I was saying when I was embodied. So I attempted to assist in this manner. Besides, I can be a clearer mirror for you in this form.

Why would you keep trying? Why is my healing so important?

A pause in Fadima's response seemed to occur, as if she were searching for the right words to say. Maybe as she had done in the past.

I think our lives are about growing and healing. If not, we keep making some of the same mistakes and carrying the same wounds into our next embodiment. You can ignore or disregard the comments of others, like pulling off the top of a weed. But if you don't remove the taproot, they simply spread, even widening the weed patch.

How do I remove the taproot? How do I eliminate the weed so such comments do not further tenderize the wound?

You must heal the wound at its source, the original infection. It sometimes requires emotional surgery, getting to the seedbed of the contamination. And you can't do that without disturbing it. That's all your client and reviewer are doing, touching your wound. As long as the infection remains, it will continue to spread. Their stroke in you is to remind you of some necessary healing. Go to the source. Heal the wound that informs you of the belief that you are not enough. Not good enough. Not lovable. That there is nothing of value inside. Heal that wound inside yourself. Then when people emotionally touch your manner of therapy or writing, you can assess whether there is value in their feedback without all the hurt you experience now.

Dylan felt tears water his eyes. A few drops roll down his cheek. Tears of relief rather than pain. Water for the healing, not just covering the wound.

Yes, your are correct. I do need to heal this. And not wait for later or some other embodiment. But how? What do I cure the infection? Dylan pleads.

To begin, thank it for the reminder. Be in gratitude for your awareness. Then love it into transition. Love it into the opportunity for change. Shine your loving light on the fundamental shift to being enough. Being love itself. And once you feel that, you are never the same. Until you forget. And that is an opportunity to remember again.

Dylan allowed Fadima's recommendation to seep into his entire being.

Why would he want to let let go of this life because someone could not see who he was inside? Why would he give up everything for someone who could not appreciate what he offered. But Fadima saw it. She recognized him and provided support to become even more.

OK, I get it. Now is the time to remedy the cause. To restore my health. For people can provide useful feedback if I don't get caught up in reoccurring pain. I know your are correct. And I'm tired of the hurt and pain. I have had enough of that. Given my experiences with you and the support you share, the alternative becomes so much greater. So much fuller and more meaningful to me. Thank you!

Could Dylan hear a smile on Fadima's face? He didn't know how. But he became certain it emerged.

Crossroads
By Geoffrey K. Leigh and Marianne Lyon

She slumped into her overstuffed chair, a scowl on her face from their most recent argument. He thumped down the hall towards his office, smoke billowing from his ears. The tension in the living room began to settle into the walls and furniture, unable to penetrate the recent refinish on the hardwood floors, tried as it might.

He typically would attempt to remain in a conversation, hoping everything would smooth out between them. But this one spiraled quickly beyond either spouse's control. His heart thumps against his chest, his face mirrors the red roses outside their window. As he considers what to do next, no reasonable option manifests.

Her arm tires from the weight of her head, begging a shift in her position. While her movement relieves minor pressure, the heaviness of her heart still searches for a release. She fails to identify a conversation in their 15 years of marriage that became this intense   blaming   hurtful. Nasty comments emerged as frequently and emphatically as his. At the moment, there appears no remorse, though she desires it to emerge.

Alone in her dim lighted office, she looks around at precious collectables. What adventures they have shared together. Tapestries from Belgium knit themselves on a wall. Prayer beads incant sacred times in Nepal. Her poetry books clutched together on a lone shelf nudge her closer. Poetry has always sung answers to life questions. She bids verse now to express this critical moment   her deep desire for remorse to emerge. Her slightly trembling hands open her to a poem she fashioned so long ago.

> Is love brazen like the sun
> when one looks through lacy branches
> at yellow lit hills
>
> Or is it hidden behind teary eyes

> trembling hands wrapping around
> a suffering friend

She looks out her window   considers the ancient oak that proceeds with a calm acceptance when doves fashion a nest in its wrinkled branches. The dove shares his with a lifetime mate singing from the elbow of bark abiding in the joy of a coo.

Don't know who queried her   the oak   the dove   but she asks herself about the verb abide.

> What is this verb abide
> Is it a muscular submission
> I steeple my fingers
> Caress   attend to my heart-voice

She has no remedy accept to invite herself to just allow her fragmented self to consider the oak   how it continues its bemused task where nothing but the wind barbers its bows. Linger with the doves when a silence appears after they incant a sublime twilight hymn. Can this emptiness she holds be an abiding compass leading her home into his arms   showing him patience and abiding love like a tree in the wind?

A blank note pad beckons her pencil. She picks it up to see what might emerge next if she continued to transcribe her experience.

> Is there any room for volition
> If my heart relaxes and eases
> What comes if my roots hold fast
> As the breeze of words filters through
> branches   around my oak self trunk
> Might astounding bird-of-paradise
> land and sing on bough once more

A deep inhale pauses her scribbles as the heart agonizes over words that arouse battle scars and reinvigorate body pains. Yet   hazy sun shines through the dissipating storm   languidly dampening the strongest wounds. The oak survived. Hope abides between the layers of cambium and sapwood. Just under the surface the light expands.

The rageful tears dry on his hot cheek and neck skin. He pens his words of indignation randomly across the page. The ache tautens his neck   stomach   intestines. His mind begins to muddle words. Now   a cloud begins to soften the edges.

He hadn't intended to be forceful   demanding   correcting all she expressed. The internal weeping begins to tenderize his organs   allows a relaxing of the argument's grip. Rage mutates into loss. His arm reaches for his guitar. He strums. His fingers change chords. Finally he settles on a song he wrote. The inner and outer tears reemerge.

But the song of long ago doesn't sing what he is feeling. A new song begs to be fashioned. He strums and plays with familiar chords. The yearning journeys him to a deeper wanting. A melody has not arrived   but through his tears he can see her face. The wanting becomes words through each sob.

He longs to compose a new feverish love song   sing it to her   watch her agate blue eyes flicker open   himself inside of them   her astonishing smile charms him   lays warm on him. He wants to write a fierce love song with a raw opening legato like years   days   hours together when minutes slow down   hungry seconds linger.

He wants to write a fairytale love song of pianissimo evenings gazing out bedroom window at moon and sun   one rising   the other setting   blending into strangeness like dreaming.

He closes his tearing eyes   tries to conjure a melodic tremor   will a romantic verse   but he hears her pass by the closed door   out to the backyard. Through his half-opened window he thinks he hears a laughing fortissimo over the pickets with a neighbor when suddenly a lento of silence intrudes. He begins to fashion a possible lyric that too becomes stunned when her percussive stride drums through the front door   down echoing hall   bids him open his wetted eyes.

She knocks   then gently opens the closed door. His glare fixes on her halfmoon grin. Could it be that her smile has found their once shared sustained passion? Her grin walks her closer. Her lips staccato-touch him. He lifts his chin andante begs for repetitions.

Ode to Her Grin

Out of steadfast sorrow
she grins
a glowing grin
a lighthouse
beacon
beckoning
even though
inevitable future storm
may drive them high
higher   away
from glimmering shore

Out of steadfast sorrow
she grins
a gallant grin
brave   perfect
a constellation
just born
in velvet sky
her grin
a generous grin
dripping hidden honey
nectar   sweet delight
sugars his eyes
candies his open heart.

4TH EPISODE

Poetry is a deal of joy and pain and wonder with a dash of the dictionary.

— Kahlil Gibran

A question to consider during this episode:

What might you write about if you choose to embrace pain and joy in the same piece?

5th Episode
Resilience in Times of Terror

If I feel physically as if the top of my head were taken off, I know it's poetry.

— Emily Dickinson

Question to consider during this episode:

What does fear smell like?
What does resilience feel like?

A Tender Moment
By Marianne Lyon

It was a day of sudden war   an attack by terrorists   A day when nothing made sense in the coldness of cruelty   A Cartel planned operation   An outrage against humanity   A day when mouths fell open in speechless disbelief   People lost in gray confusion   intense destruction   You didn't have to be in Ecuador to feel the horror   to feel broken into pieces or smashed in darkness and rubble   Ecuador moaned and wept sick with the pain of grief   distraught with biting anger   We will survive but never forget

Dark Hours
By Marianne Lyon

Dark hours
crumple   press
no escape from their crush
how merciless the fist of grief
how strong the squeeze
how difficult to believe we'll survive

Today   it is enough
to offer a simple song
wordless   melodic
how momentarily grateful
I am to hum this sonorous offering
jagged breath carrying shock away

Shut in
By Marianne Lyon

Will I remember the darkness twenty years from now that held us hostage on wings of terror as an evil plot played out on innocent streets   TV station   local establishments   Survivors of that awful day will asked why we stand with an uncertain future   with God at our side   an angel at our back   we still see love is possible where hate reigns flooding caverns of hopelessness with streams of forgiveness   light on the other side of darkness.

Clouds puff in morning sky
tired eyes squint at gloomy grey
lone statue of Jesus looms over
I lower myself onto unmade bed
my room   my cell
car horns neigh

There are long moments
when life falls away
and your own name falls away and
everything you thought you knew
falls away   and for a moment
you know yourself only
as whatever it is
your whole body trembles
with the eternity of it
and you quiver
as if struck by the great hand
you   a tuning fork
becoming pure tone
more vibration than flesh
a human-shaped resonator
tuned to the frequency

of fear itself
though later you might try
to dissect what happened
in that moment you're too shaken
to wonder how or why
you simply are
this frightful unfolding
you tremble like a song

How
By Marianne Lyon

Bid Rumi to harmonize me through these fear filled days   He reminds me when I vocalize from my soul   I will feel a melodious river moving in me   Nudges me ignore thoughts that grab me fearful and despaired   that degrade me back towards dread   And for a long moment I forget safety   Live where I fear to live   become notorious   Sing when I am broken open   Sing when I take the bandage off   Sing in the middle of battle   Sing in the blood   I want to canary like birds   Not worry about who hears   or what they think   Dear poets   there is a candle in our hearts ready to be kindled   There is a song in our souls ready to be lilted   You feel it   hear it   don't you

Ripening*
By Marianne Lyon

I trundle forward
when so much is bitterly fragile
I tremble like an animal
caught in a field of terror
Unsettled moments like these
I invite poetry to blossom inside paradox
Hard now to believe in patience
hard to trust transformation   hard to surrender
to the choreography of troubled life
How do I turn myself into something I'm not
The ripest   sweetest grapes
make the strongest wine
Whatever is sweetest inside
now begs to shine through me
I still feel a current of emptiness yet
as I fashion this short poem
I am learning to trust
my inevitable ripening

If the drink is bitter, turn yourself to wine.
—Rainer Maria Rilke, from *"Sonnets to Orpheus 2, 29," trans.*

Genuine poetry can communicate before it is understood.

— T. S. Eliot

In Lockdown Conversation
By Marianne Lyon

Gold morning fractures into tiny rainbows   Bite pink-cheeked orb   slurp sweet juice   Come   sit a spell under Grandpa's apple-tree-paradise like we did as kids   Back then we mimed to converse   went deep inside each other's heart Endlessness lived there   Taste his courageous smile   feel rugged pain he breathed into polished wooden flute   tooting a salty tune for us and framed-faded photos of old country faces   Kiss work-worn hands   His eyes wide at their turning on sunken-weary lap but knees still invite us bounce   yelp   ride a palomino   Can you match Gramp's irresistible roguish ha-ha's   his slight flicker of amusement inside blazing blue eyes   Will you choose courage   imitate his tender twinkle when constellations of disappointment bolt into your sky   When fear is so loud your arms become mapped in chills   dive with me into redeeming endlessness

Daunting siren shrieks
enter me   become me
become a synapse to dark shadows
on deserted streets
become my racing pulse
become boiling blood
become jagged breath
And in this way   the more I listen
the more I am witched
wearing another body
from another time   place
It is no small thing to converse
with staccato locution
Sometimes I swim in its wild stormy
lexicon   Sometimes I break
on a jagged shore
Others are wrecking balls

     that turn to rubble   all I thought I knew
            Grateful for your presence
                in our prison room
            How fleeting it is   any grasp
              of who we are   This is why
           hour after hour minute by minute
             I welcome your conversings
          Even when they are not easy to hear
                amid the bleating horns
                 I love who I become
              in those flummoxed moments
           when vulnerable me abides with you

              Even the ancient oak
                   proceeds
                with calm acceptance
            when doves fashion a nest
              in its wrinkled branches.

Sometimes I yearn to live in enduring countenance to allow darkness to deepen sit with the moon newly swollen   The dove shares his roost with a lifetime mate singing from an elbow of bark   abiding in the joy of a coo   What is this verb abide   Is it a muscular submission

                I steeple my fingers
                bid you keep to me
                     for a bit

What   you say   you are languidly in hope   winnowing in dread   a large patch of emptiness   I have no remedy accept to invite you just allow your fragmented self to consider the oak   how it continues its bemused task where nothing but the wind barbers its bows   Linger with the doves when a silence appears after they incant a sublime twilight hymn

                 Can that emptiness

you hold
be an abiding compass
leading you home to your nest
showing you patience
like a tree in the wind

The Unbroken
By Marianne Lyon

Walls of courage I thought would shelter   are whipped down by merciless
terrorists

I'm too weary
to rebuild them
Enough   I shout,
my voice nothing
inside the fear
Go away
I whimper.

Yet I am still here   What is it that caresses me alive   Whatever it is

it's harder now
to see myself
not married to it
When I wail
it is what wipes my tears
When I cannot lift
myself form the chair
it takes on a human shape
and raises me up

A Tuning Fork
By Marianne Lyon

Not Anything   not the deep alleys of dark thought that unravel life into disorder not the unbreaking loneliness inside a sorrow that can't talk   not the twisting wind that howls up forbidding me to get blissfully lost in afternoon walk   nor the president who rips my nerves to rags   Not anything will recast my deep affection for you, my fellow humans at our border, inflight from terror into bitter cruelness or for blessed you, my dear Ecuador friends, my beloved husband or for you, Mary Oliver, your poems make gratitude my Holy Communion. Or for you, my precious dog and the walks through the fields heated by high sun vibrating the air or for you, wizened woman whose face is beginning to wrinkle as a dried leaf my precious self.

>   There are long moments
>   when life falls away
>   and your own name falls away and
>   everything you thought you knew
>   falls away   and for a moment
>   you know yourself only
>   as whatever it is
>   your whole body trembles
>   with the eternity of it
>   and you quiver
>   as if struck by the great hand
>   you   a tuning fork
>   becoming pure tone
>   more vibration than flesh
>   a human-shaped resonator
>   tuned to the frequency
>   of fear itself
>   though later you might try

to dissect what happened
in that moment you're too shaken
to wonder how or why
you simply are
this frightful unfolding
you tremble like a song

White Cane
By Valli Ferrell

When I carry the white cane,
    I am redefined,
        visually branded to the world.
I abhor the cane.
It confirms the uneasy reality
    that I am legally blind.
The white cane is so absolute.
I am not totally blind —
just blind enough
    that I cannot see a face
    read a book
    drive a car
Blind enough
to need a white cane.

I straddle two worlds
    Blind
    Sighted
with membership in neither,
a nether land that confuses everyone,
    including me.

I lament my need for the cane.
It confirms my blindness.
It alters my self-image.
    Shouts my disability —
    it steals my privacy,
    my anonymity.

Everyone notices me,

which is   of course
the point of the white cane.

Seeing a white cane
    stops the car,
    clears my path,
    evokes offers of assistance.

Vanity keeps me from the cane.
It is not a hip accessory.
I try holding the cane
like a hiking stick.
Who am I fooling with the red-tipped white cane?
I am tempted to use it as a weapon
    against off leash dogs
    that startle me.
Instead, I try for elegance.
Can I be the coolest, most graceful woman with a cane?

Fear keeps me from the cane.
Those who know me as a sighted person
    may shun me as a blind person.
Those who don't know me
    may label me
    that blind woman.

I am a mess of contradiction.
I channel my mantra,
    Breathe
    Peace
    Be still
Inner stillness helps me cope
outer stillness helps me listen
to discern safety from threat.
There are days   I confess,

when I see less well than other days.
When I am tired
of the waking work of seeing—
    interpreting murky visuals
    conflicting sounds
    jumbled words with missing parts
        unknown pieces of mail
        misplaced medication
        favorite lipstick.

I avoid using the cane.
    I rationalize —
I am familiar with my surroundings.
I don't need the cane for this brief errand.
    I can pass for sighted,
    can go unnoticed
    just this once.

I deny my need for the cane,
but when I nearly collide
with a passing cyclist
that I did not hear approaching,
was startled by the whoosh of air,
the whisper of contact,
the sharp cry of the rider
at our near miss —
I accept,
finally,
the absolute necessity
of the white cane.

It's All Temporary
By Kathryn Santana Goldman

"Nothing is normal here." ~ Emilie Lygren

Basel Cell Carcinoma was the diagnosis.
The easiest to treat - they said.
We had queasy expectations
for a quick treatment and recovery.

Five hours later, with a skin graft,
covered by a pliable cast,
we head home clutching
your wound care instructions.

Simple paint-by-number guides,
dressing changes twice a day.
I cleansed and covered, watching
your body forgive and repair.

Like a patched and re-inflated tire,
we rolled forward, listing slightly.
The journey we traveled
offered no permanent destination.

Six weeks later, I wake before you.
A wisp of sunlight reveals
the soft curve of a smile,

worry temporarily released
from your face and my heart,
like the scar receding from view.

Abide with Grief & Joy
By Marianne Lyon

Even the ancient oak proceeds with calm acceptance when doves fashion a nest in its wrinkled branches. Sometimes I yearn to live in enduring countenance. Allow darkness to deepen.
Sit with the moon newly swollen. The dove shares his roost.
when a lifetime mate, singing from an elbow of bark abiding in the joy of coo.

What is this verb abide
Is it a muscular submission
I steeple my fingers
bid you keep to me for a bit.

What, you say, you are languidly in hope, winnowing in dread a large patch of emptiness? I have no remedy accept to invite you just allow your fragmented self to consider the oak how it continues its bemused task where nothing but the wind barbers its bows. Linger with the doves when a silence appears after they incant a sublime twilight hymn.

Can that emptiness you hold
be an abiding compass
leading you home to your nest
showing your patience
like a tree in the wind

Ecclesiastical Rose
By Geoffrey K. Leigh

Sometimes when I fancy the sweet floral scent of the dazzling red rose
stabs remind me of thorns concealed behind the leaves that turn light into life
and nourish the honey spiced notes wafting in the breeze calling my attention
and desire for the many ways petals fragrance my life and being

My early religious rose enticed me to attempt a life within theological dogma
determined primarily by men ordained by men to pose as divine servants for all
creating pontifical protocol that spawn thorns of arrogance, judgments, lies
upon transgression dispense the pain of disgrace, self-doubt, self-decimation

Shame and guilt facilely spew forth on judgment's wings from pulpit and print
intending to shore adherence by followers with core hopes of eternal salvation
despite sentient pain from inner thorns attempting to prompt greater devotion
believing words accurate, truthful, instead of control and economic hoarding

Over time the doctrinal barbs become recognized as extrinsic to my being, my core
not an inherent part of my virtue or worth, but inserted by the judgmental clergy
who propagate rules, beliefs, promises of eternal life, connection to divine while
masquerading egoistic drives that inflate their salience, eminence, prosperity

Do rules, promises attributed to deistic origin make ecclesiastics sacred sources
If creation is divine, does inspiration not take me closer to celestial provenance
At times, ingenuity turns on theistic structure and reveals the illusion of hallowed
underpinnings that point more directly to faux idol than divine representative

Thorns converted to soft petals of love's core in self and ripen into guidelines of
self-trust, care for essence and heart, embrace self as equal to other and vise versa
reorienting theological intention from the inside out, aware that if divine subsists
in all, our closest juncture resides within as interconnections extend to the whole

Poetry is when an emotion has found thought and the thought has found words.

— **Robert Frost**

A question to consider during this episode:

Which famous poet would you write to who winged you up and you flew?

6th Episode
Ekphrastic Poetry and Prosetry

A creative life is an amplified life. It's a bigger life, a happier life, an expanded life, and a hell of a lot more interesting life.

— Elizabeth Gilbert

A question to consider during this episode:

Choose a painting. How would you describe it without using the sense of sight

Girl with a Pearl Erring by Johannas Vermeer

Painting by Vermeer
By Marianne Lyon

The lamp of her intimate gaze gleams hungry questions that probe our luminous nature, radiant as iridescent pearl swinging from her ear.

In fierce black ground the lamp of her intimate gaze gleams. Darkness ponders our luminous nature, radiant as iridescent pearl. Seeking brilliant answers in fierce black ground earthly desire and divine luminescence bathe in pool of darkness pondering these question entreating answers to her shining lips a passionate kiss or prophecy, earthly desire or divine luminescence

> I surrender
> to hungry queries
> passionate kisses
> or prophecy
> pondering ineffable
> while
> the lamp of her intimate gaze
> gleams

Friends & Lovers, a digital collage by Kirk Hinshaw

Who Decides?
By Geoffrey K. Leigh

Who gets to judge what love is and what love isn't?
Can we comprehend such affection with limited scope?
Do we defer responsibility for the verdict beyond this moment, place, time?

If adult hearts are expressing unconditional caring, mutual supportive touch,
kindness and affection, am I so blind not to notice enormous adoration?
Do I avoid observation of deep external connection? Do I disconnect part of me?
Is what I refuse to acknowledge on the outside? Or internal?
Is the closed heart mine?

I see no human harm when adults love one another.
I sense no closed hearts when one reaches out to caress with adoring embrace.
I surmise that passion and intimacy create greater connection.

What I do experience is how judgment separates us rather than brings us closer.
My own heart closes down when I adjudicate another's affection.
Is judgment what love isn't?

Lenticular Cloud
By John Petraglia

Photo by John Petraglia

A rare lenticular cloud hovers
like a flat rounded river stone
above my Napa home at early dusk
where the dark Japanese maple
splays in architectural grandeur.

I wonder who named these alto cumuli
Lenticulars, lens-like, lentil-shaped?
How the name came to the science?
Why the pale edged cloud
hanging saucerly in stable evening air
below the hillside moves me?
Why the newly risen moon
lends unneeded eeriness
to this domestic halo,
as I pause a few minutes
before entering my home.

And then it is gone.
Not the sky drama, twilit singular cloud
you may have seen in a photo
haunting lonely Fuji, snowy Kilimanjaro.
But my transient admiration, wonder
for the awesome firmament display tonight.
So easily replaced by the heavenly embrace
of my newly pregnant daughter
visiting me with her own supernatural grace.

Embrace
By Marianne Lyon

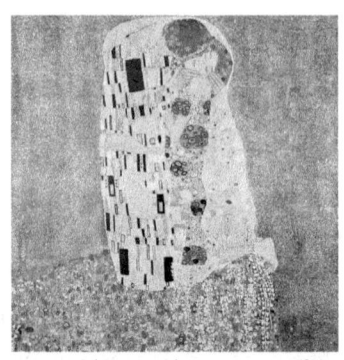

The Kiss by Gustav Klint

Divide between us
six feet   give or take
these dark days of
physical distancing

No longer hugs or kisses
normal social greeting
we stand back   space apart
masked   trying to protect

I yearn for the time
lurking virus disappears
from our midst   normalcy
returns hope   not despair.

Will warmth radiating from
physical animals we are
be lost to collective memory
When can we embrace

Wide Open
By Valli Ferrell

I.
1946~ An attic room, a garret high
where tremulous strains of Piaf drift
la-la-la vie en rose
lovebirds coo, enjoy the view
bare bottom, nightie slipping,
a tousled brunette on buoyant tiptoe,
leans out the open window
watching her lover go.
A languid twist of sheet trails,
An aimless wisp of stocking surrendered,
saucy red heels discarded
in last night's dark.
Does she spy him in the busy street,
hold his parting smile?
Will he return with *café au lait*
a tarte aux pommes—
sweetest of apples to share before devouring
each other in morning's golden light?

Attic Room by Louis Icart

II.
1981~ Paris flea market, a painting spied,
A young brunette discovers
another brunette   serendipitous—
her twin, her kin; she is certain.
The clock fixed at 7:50,
her waking hour to the minute
The *come fuck me* mules,
her own in pink with ostrich feathers.
Her body stirs

at the single stocking
draped as it is,
The pleasure game she plays,
played out here, on the canvas.
Her spirited heart flies
into a future unclouded;
years beyond blitz and blackout,
the window beckons, wide open,
life unrationed.

Petunias by Georgia O'Keeffe

Painting by Georgia O'Keeffe
By Marianne Lyon

Songs held me in her garden   shaped my life from the inside   voices purring from moist grass sometimes so faint   I thought it was wind   One day I heard grandma's petunias   No words at first   Only deep purple yielding velvet   world as a flower   I sang back   sounds I have forgotten   don't use anymore   the flowers trilled about growing with a touch of wildness   I was entwined to their voices   verses would drop over and over   like layering of petals they began to reap words out of me   ditties with changeable words   reckless, yearning to be fully grown   in bloom   Dusk sweeps down like a shawl   petunias given over to kale   I return to the songs   outrageous fantasies   step in them   and rest there is nothing else   I wonder if O'Keefe's petunias sang to her about subtle radiant hues   hearts filled with sunshine   the vast cosmos   the unspeakable.

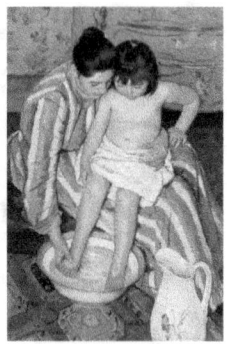
*The Child's Bath by
Mary Cassatt*

The Child's Bath
By Kathryn Santana Goldman

I study our reflection.
She has my hair, my eyes,
my skin - before womanhood.

Her toes ripple the water.
Our images blur.
We pause and wait to re-appear.

A sweet in-between moment.
I inhale my daughter's child-scent,
hold my breath and memorize her innocence.

Her gentle laughter,
like a warm evening breeze,
caresses my heart.

We linger as I watch the sun
move across her face,
reminding me this time is fleeting.

Great things are done by a series of small things brought together.

— Vincent Van Gogh

Mushroom Village
By Geoffrey K. Leigh

Rock Mushrooms, photograph by Geoffrey K. Leigh

Propped tall motionless statures
perfectly balanced tilted hats
patiently waiting for cover of darkness
to loosen stone veneer
brew magical life of laughter
shifting dance positions and interactions
until sunlight hardens external surface
solid   unmovable
awaiting moonlight shadows
again freeing inner music and joy

*Woman with Raven by
Pablo Picasso*

Raven
By Marianne Lyon

High in heron proud cedar
a raven pulls a glance from me
obsidian eyes, a prophet

I consider him closely   try to figure every
brush stroke of him   elegant   strikingly restrained
abides like a Moses   cocks unruly look
an epiphany boils   something hungry in his tilt
dips his beak   finds my stare again
complains like a cranky gate   gruff story unspools then
gathers up like a storm   dives down from his high wire
stilted legs maneuver   tricky footing on forest flooor

scavenges around relentlessly
fusses over brittle twigs
a feisty old woman
stiff in the knees

squints at tangled ground   squawks the gist of it

peers up to his majestic fiefdom   in deep séance then
evaporates from tedious pecking   a midnight phantom
diamond gleam of him   a palisade of silence between us
         unmoored   impromptu zigzags
            disappears as if gulped

Fume D'Ambergris
By John Petraglia

Fume D'Ambergis by John Singer Sargent

She embraces
the wafting, sultry scents
of waxen ambergris and myrrh
rising from a hammered argent
Moroccan censer.
The sweet and musty scents
redolent of love's afterglow
rise slowly in the corner
of the antechamber
aside the beveled shaft
of an ancient pillar.
Inlaid with blue jewels
and Moorish filigree
two triangular silver pendants
Gather her ivory caftan to her shoulders
easily loosed
in moments of princely passion.
She reverently hoods the white fold
Of her veil as a sacred headdress
in an erotic capture that shows no skin
save for dark forearms
shadowed face, carmine lips.
Surrounded by sun-bleached stone
she stands on a Persian rug
woven with black, buck and golden threads
tenting herself in a final perfuming ritual
before moving to the harem chamber.

Night Sky-People
By Marianne Lyon

Some radiate out
like spokes of a wheel
Some walk alone
their luster conceal
Some cluster close
protect their young
Some glow only
in their native tongue
Some meteor bright stage
like Fred Astaire
Some duet with John Legend
igniting a prayer
Some glint sacred visions
of the Great Beginning
Some howl, ablaze wildly
old fairytales unfolding
Some fading-luster walkers
Some pulsing playpens
Some falling-star Billionaires
Some poor chanting "Amens"
Some jewels just baptized
all shiny and new
Some fashion rhyming verses
other poets-stars think taboo

Starry Night by Vincent Van Gogh

Einstein's Sky
By Marianne Lyon

Dear Albert   did you really say
"science without religion is lame"
Did you repose under constellations
hour-less nights   no calculations
no formulas
knowing infinity lives in cosmic sparkle
hoping to stir eons of boundless wonderment

Starry Night by Jean-Francois Millet

When in deep contemplation   did a welling-up
ferry you into timeless paradise   priests call heaven
I ask you if this sacramental   delirious suspension
could be but a black hole   final grave   consuming us

Tonight   blackness swallows me
Imbibed into inky abyss   reshaped
miraculously turned inside out   silent

I wonder of my finality   earth's extinction
the fate of pondering
When you luxuriated under constellations
hour-less nights   did you implore God
that this luxury   not be something
time forced you leave behind

Did you write a verse   incant an intersession
invite *tempus fugit* back   over and over

Fly a Kite
By Marianne Lyon

La Cometa (The Kite) by Francisco de Goya

I bear up under dark center of pain
can no longer see through it
when current of something other
than my trouble unfurls an understanding
like a flower blown out of hands
of someone grasping
and my mind floats
can see light   weightless
for the first time in months
howling grief falls mute
I feel whole in a new way
as if the breaking I'd been through
has salved over open wounds
I can't name this other than to say
I have moved through something difficult
that is finally opened
all this bearing up   bearing down
there is a touch of eternity in the air
I am lifted like a kite on perfumed wind
that my young self once chased

Love Is In The Air
By Geoffrey K. Leigh

Photo by Geoffrey K. Leigh

As I spotted dried tendrils
heart shape created
on top trellis catch wire
I wondered if love was in the air

I realized it was in the sun
warming my face with early rays
and afternoon heat
warming my aching back

It appeared in a murder of crows
as they cooperate in search of food
or the mud left in low vineyard spots
water still seeping into aquifers

It showed up in laughter
of two colleagues while working
and the cirrus and cumulous clouds
as they paint designs in the sky

I felt it in the dormant vines
taking shape for new growth
my hands carefully wrapping canes
with promise of bud break and fruit

I discerned in the sky and ground
wires   birds   canes   people
I discovered it in the air and me
when I take time to notice

Poetry is an echo asking a shadow to dance.

— **Carl Sandburg**

Question:

How will your emotions find words to map your world?

7th Episode
Prosetic Art

*Don't wait for inspiration.
It comes while working.*

— Henri Matisse

A question to consider during this episode:

Imagine someone who doesn't know you are watching him/her. Describe the image

Back to my Garden
By Marianne Lyon

Tonight
I relish the chance
to miss you
to miss you so much
I surrender into the missing
the way your roses surrendered
into my hands   and caressed me back
until my world was ambrosial
whiff of loving   and the pungence
was everything   I want to stroll into my garden
that still grows in me
and disappear in it
let it take me completely
I want it   and
I don't want it
I love this broken world
want to leave   yet
I want to be so in service
to aromatically love
the suffering
that there is
nothing left of me
but rampant
self-shattering love
I want everything but love
to burn to ash.
Want everything but love to be blown away   Want all that is left is my feral heart
still opening   though it seems it couldn't possibly break open any more
yet I marvel as it opens again   again into how is it possible   more perfumed love

Burying Ground
By Marianne Lyon

I reverence this morning out kitchen window   grove of pines alchemies
me to family tombs cemeteried decades on haloed hill

I exit
from
shadow
thinking
Remember   how Grandpa
vigored his daily walks   How
Gram magiced every X"mas
Eve with
unexpected
fairy surprises

Pilgrim
myself
back to
Dad's
reverent eyes in incensed sanctuary
On way home from Mass   hear me
hum Sanctus   He croons back
"This Little
Light of
Mine"

Can't
forget
Mom's
topaz eyes   Smile threads
on her face Her galaxy of love
still
starlight's
my days

Morning splendors the room   I brushstroke these family memories
Begin to page my thoughts for you to read Grin lines my face "This little light of mine I'm going to let it shine

get it?*
like a lich-
tenstein thought
balloon the question
hangs over *comedian*
a readymade sculpture
that's one banana duct-
taped to a wall— only
rembrandt could render
expressions on the faces
clustered all around the
yellow rot-freckled grin
goofy fruit of maurizio
cattelan's puckish brain
that plucks him a sweet
two-hundred-forty gees—
who says money doesn't
grow on trees? Taking a
cue from the top banana,
a wannabe performance
artist steps out from the
bunch, peels tape and
objet d'art & just for
laughs (& just a little
taste of fame) takes
a gorilla-sized bite
— the punch
line

By Michael Waterson

*Grateful acknowledgment is made to Winged Penny Review where a version of this poem first appeared. Imagine the poem with yellow background.

The Apple Tree in Grandpa's Eden*
By Marianne Lyon

Crisp summer afternoon
seeds spill from pine birdhouse
chipped picket fence encloses **crimson** rhubarb
spindly chives reach out to **sunlight orb**   a chance at freedom
You nap in windowless shed
light *juices* through open door introducing
faded pictures of *tart* relatives in circular frames
Musty wool   fermenting *appliness* grabs my breath
Waltzing to the painted bench under your love-tended tree
You sings *edible* words I almost understand
Honey sounds in a minor key   *delicious* melodies
whistle from your wooden flute.
You offer me a *fruit*   wash then dry it
on your *cinnamon* shirt   it shines
You and Dad share the bench
drink homemade *cider*
talk about fishing
dandelion season
I bite into *crunchy* gift
imagine grandma's
apple sauce and ***streusel***
Will birds to light
on the birdhouse perch
then quietly sneak
into shed's silence
I conjure tales of those unhappy people on the wall
Didn't realize how much store I set on these afternoons
I yearn for you to wash a pome   glisten it on your belly

*Imagine the bold & italicized words are red apples in an otherwise green tree with a brown base from the last three lines.

Open the Rusty Lid*

I adore yellow roses   climbing star jasmine
Detest giant hogweeds,   musk thistle, cheatgrass
Soft jazz soothes me while golden oldies reminisce former romances
Heavy metal hurts my ears and stiffens, agitates, roils my body and soul
Invited pleasant plants☐ sounds nourish, the ground and near atmosphere
Invasive vegetation and harsh tones become decomposition for future fuel
Any can be invitation or compost, enhancement or uneasiness, soft or hard
None is inherent in the herbage or composition, an organic part of objects
Determination lies more in our senses, gut, experiences, brain, and heart
When I prohibit, verdict the outcome, separation, hierarchy ensues
When others become diminished, I can feel more competent
But when I face the issue, the blindness oft disappears
Internal shifts increasingly create external change
When love streams internally, it easily includes
Change the world, and all around us
people, plants, earth, separation
Follow Glaude's suggestion
Love will open the
rusty lid of our
hearts.

By Geoffrey K. Leigh

* Inspired by James Baldwin and <u>Begin Again</u> by Eddie S. Glaude Jr. Imagine the title and entire poem in red letters.

Poetry is language at its most distilled and most powerful.

— **Rita Dove**

Come, Sit By Me
By Kathryn Santana Goldman

Only when it is dark enough can you see the stars - MLK

Come sit alongside me.
Empty your hands, hold mine.

Let us remember the stories
underneath our scars

shudder at common themes,
laugh and, maybe, cry.

There was the time
you sheltered me from

the slicing beacon of light
casting shadows on my heart.

You allowed my tears to flow
until my breath returned.

>Come, sit next to me. We can gaze through
>   the charcoal evening sky. Spy the glittering bits

>   of celestial bodies cascading
>   hope across the universe.

>   Before we return to stardust,
>   Come, sit by me

>   and let me love you.

```
        L                    H*
         I                    O
          G                    U
           H                    S
            T                    E
```

                She
              listened
          it was very still
       cricket   was over
     children in their baths
    only the sound of the sea
   she looked at the steady light
    the pitiless   remorseless
  which was so much her   which
   was so little her   which had
  her at its beck and call   for all
   that she thought   watching with
   fascination   hypnotized   as if it
  we're stroking   with silver fingers
some sealed vessel in her brain   whose bursting
   would flood her   with delight
  she had known happiness   exquisite happiness
   intense happiness   it silvered the rough waves
  a little more brightly   rolled in waves of pure lemon
ecstasy burst in her eyes   waves of pure delight   raced over the floor of her mind
       it is enough   it is enough

By Marianne Lyon

Found poem, Virginia Wolf- Lighthouse

```
          r
       p e
      P a
       t o
      P e n
```

I put pen to paper   draft initial thoughts
Wonder where the head will lead
No   not just the mind   what other parts assist
Creation   beauty   express previously unstated
A pause   a thought   another possibility
Maybe my gut will add more insight tonight
I know not where inspiration dwells
Reception is all that matters
Increasingly I trust the open acceptance
allowing access to what is most sublime
Avoid the drop into open abyss   lost
at times in doubt   inadequacy   shame
I crawl to the edge   see the magnificence beyond
How do I surrender to the sources of originality   inspiration
Then I peer to what holds me back   nothing materializes
I buoy myself up   inhale   then puff out
As I let go and write   mindless intention
Words   phrases   ideas manifest
Get out of my own way and listen   just open
I allow   surrender   pen to paper
More than I can use authors itself

By Geoffrey K. Leigh

Main Street
By Marianne Lyon

I Venture
Out tonight
Dryness polishes
Enlarges the stars
Lightening my steps

They
Appear
At   Some carry empty buckets
All   others carry nothing at all

A thrice-widow clutches
Her worn Old Testament   *Hours*
On Our   Some jackets grow larger
       Winter after winter
       Some downcast and
Silk   Some in sad pinchers
Road
Through

One gazes at me   *Town*
As if she'd never seen
A young girl's eyes lifted
To the stars   a swinging gate   *Only*   Some carry necessities
Tributary   Some carry loss of their job
To   Some their loss of reason
       Heading for a dark saloon

Some thin as an I   *Shoes*
Some humped like an f
Jawlines a U
Twisted strand of grace
strung together into verses

Food

                        God

Main Street fashions   with human attention
At its highest reach   we know as poetry

Wine Memories
By Marianne Lyon

A graceful swirl of Cabernet dervishes
me down to Grandpa's cellar   dark
shrouded   pungent   sweaty barrels
stained red   Coquettish   swirl of
Chardonnay   and   I feel his velvet
eyes smile through legs transparent
dancing around the glass   I sip
Pinot Noir   recline impromptu
in Provence vineyard   Taste
lacy flowers   waltzing
with
wild
fruit
disco
swirl
whiff
aerated
memories
Another sip
buttery memories still to be fermented

Poetry is my deepest health.

— **Sylvia Plath**

A question to consider for your writing:

Imagine yourself watching a concert.
Choose something to look at and contemplate.
What is the view saying to you?

8th Episode
Prosetry from Music

Poetry is one of the ancient arts, and it began as did all the fine arts, within the original wilderness of the earth.

— Mary Oliver

A question to consider during this episode:

**Play a piece of your favorite music.
What is the first thing that appears in your mind?**

From Message to Morphosis*
By Geoffrey K. Leigh and Marianne Lyon

The pace of change materialized beyond belief
from lonely encouragements providing minuscule relief
Diverse groups stressed equality for all
including commensurate opportunities   big and small
Discontinue silenced voices   end limit who can play
open opportunities in power structures   what all can say
Exclusion to be heard leave hearts chagrinned
omitted and ignored   simply shouting in the wind
Desire for inclusion in discussions and decisions
contribute to the strength of collective visions

Memory reminds how the world is a-changin'
anger wakes with each morning   now pessimism reigning
Life should know peace   instead desperation overwhelms
stealing breath from freedom   in havoc's realm
Ignorance gets planted   produce intolerance seeds
by those without conscience   division its deeds
Upset with the changes society has accepted
the dedication to destroy wants alterations rejected
But assemblies eschew the present fight to dominate
as more and more desire   inclusion to promulgate

When voices appeared to echo small halls
power structures limited modification calls
Efforts increased for social structures preserved
traditional benefits for others   not deserved
Threescore years later the conventional screamed
too much change for undeserving has been gleaned
Late majority and laggards pressed to reverse the clock

expanded roles   relationships   identity changes were crock
The fight emerged to subjugate progression
limiting tolerance   freedom   became the obsession

Come hither dear friends from so many rooms
let's share our heart stories buried in tombs
Dylan was correct with his changing song
look around   something's gone vastly wrong
We must be the change as Gandhi decreed
walking for freedom   for all are in need
Beg our leaders like Bernie to demand
he stop his ridiculous   outlandish commands
There's a Washington battle   for sure it's a-ragin'
For the times   they are a-changin'

Gather all   you who suffer   feel you have no home
together let us find our way back to shalom
Nudge our silent voices to incant a freedom song
be a hero   much responsibility accompanies us along
This land is your land   this land is mine
our country is now run by those avoiding muse-time
Dynamically pursue what you feel in open heart
understand   beneath beautiful   lives pieces of discomfort
Remember those not busy being reborn are busy dying
join us   we're a majority   dancing   lifting off   flying

Tis the majority that support reformations been made
while the holdouts jabber too much has been played
As multitudes care   include   defend
desperate power mongers continue to pretend
They claim to be advocates of poor   downtrodden
as they strangle freedoms of outcast   forgotten
When hearts realize that love includes tolerance

we finally may care about people over opulence
Breathe deeply, my friends, and apply your voice
to profoundly understand and escalate choice

* A collaborative prosetry composition inspired by *The Times They Are A-Changin'* by Bob Dylan and by Dr. Seuss.

New-New World Symphony*
By Marianne Lyon

Do you think there is anything not attached by an unbreakable chord
to everything else

When I hold this query
I hear something like music
rise steadily inside
a melodic theme
that might erupt
into wild crescendo
or maybe a slow legato
burning-spill

This dusk I walk on companion path inside my favorite time of day   thinking of
cities I have
lived—Hong Kong   Brussels   countries visited—
Zimbabwe   Congo

Remember these places
swallowed in
setting sun brilliance
how fiery-evening-miracle
ignites for everyone
so faithfully magical

I ask what if we are all but single notes trembling off stage—muted thunder
waiting to be
acknowledged harmonized   fashioned into one hallowed symphony

* Inspired by Dvorak's No. 5 "New World Symphony"

Overture
By Marianne Lyon

It's all here
    a few fleeting
        musical moment
            all here
just-planted
    seedling
        prelude of themes intertwines
            wistful free child
flourishing largely
    in sun of their arms
        See, Mom's blue-willow tea-cup
            glitters in afternoon rays

                suddenly minor dirge
                vibrates spoon on saucer
                feel myself perched
                in dark corner
                want to grab Dad's lifeless hand
                bring him back but
                only hear endless requiem
                louder more persistent

My sprouting fingers
    paint his stick figure
        in garden sandbox
            want him, miss him so
and from somewhere inside
    I begin to will
        Overture's minor melody to modulate
            into flute's healing whisper

Look, smiling-Mom draws velvet curtain
her love unspools itself
Dad appears
beaming in front row
I stride onto sun lit stage
childhood love arias
vibrate in my throat
I make a solo
wistful free entrance
for my operetta
is about to begin

Inspired by Mozart's Magic Flute Overture

Whistle*
By Marianne Lyon

He whistles through
the yards of his day
echoes charming birdsongs
whines ruckus Croatian ditties
deep in the realm of his
own melodic invention
tender toots match his swagger
from garage
lucid trills gives shape to
another project

I try to whistle   match his timbre   crinkle my lips   vary moist curl of my tongue find a crevice between front teeth   but clouds of spit skirl out   like an oscillating table fan   Insistent   I linger over a book given to whistling   relentless scores of tunes   intricate as an aria   a crush of notes fly   soar   dive   slurs dance wild tangos with haughty staccatos   Bach would be impressed that lips alone can maneuver such virtuosity and to carve   whittle   garden walk at the same time

I remember how each day
he nobly pipered home
lunch bucket swinging a steady pulse
certain in his course
his limbering form twists up narrow alley
lips purse, head tilts
I hear his signature
tight high tootle unravel
transfixed, I drop my crayons
run to the luxurious exhale

Inspired by my Dad's gift of whistling

A Soprano in Lucca
By Marianne Lyon

Lights dim   she stands smiling   I inhale stillness   when a piano glissando enters the waiting silence   her lips round   bare shoulders lean   hands dance like buoyant leaves in tender wind   my eyes close   the aria unravels like a worn sweater made new again tonight

                        words
                        undulate
                        encircle
                        spin
                        grow to
                        a crescendo
                        lift
                        pull
                        set me down
                        in a place that
                        whispers
                        surrenders me into
                        breathless quiet
                        my eyes open slowly to her smile
                        waiting for applause

* *Inspired by a soprano singing opera to an eager audience in a Lucca, Italy square*

A Letter to James Taylor*
By Marianne Lyon

James   who has felt *fire and rain, lonely times without a friend*
    Dark-themed hits   verses that vibrate lasting grief are favored
  Read   memorized   published   James   what of the joy of singing
    ourselves home   Writers now choose uncomfortable   dissonance
the yearning played over and over until we are chained in a Wagner-Never-Ending Opera   forgetting to visit hearth-warmth even for a brief moment of rest-resolution   James, are we mistaking pain as the only way to sing through life   The suffering poet's leitmotif   So   when we hear harmony   are we afraid because we haven't felt it for so long   it becomes this scary space behind a locked gate
  James   I have felt *fire and rain*   carried despair   abandonment   dipped my toes in unbearable   but I want to write about all aspects of me   I want to write about *sunny days I thought would never end*   about rising from darkness at sunrise   sinking back into bleakness at night   But James   I want to proclaim rising again the next morning   I want to compose verses about promise   sing with the sun   dawn after dawn.

*Inspired by *I've Seen Fire and I've Seen Rain*- James Taylor

Art is the elimination of the unnecessary.

— **Pablo Picasso**

Imagine*
By Marianne Lyon

I tune well-picked acoustic guitar   set up lone snare drum
roll in polished baby grand hope they received my e-mail

I don't know what time it is
sunset pinks up white capped mountains
first Joan slides in singing   *No Woman No Cry*
minutes later   Joni arrives   croons   *A Case of You*
I've looked at life from Both Sides Now repeats as
Judy lilts in   hair wispy like an angel

These songs transcend me   walk me through my teens
confront me with a recreation of bygone times

Joni suggests   *Let's jam*
Improvise a song about now
solo words make an entrance,
gentle tunes slide around
Judy giggles Not as easy as it was
back then

Joan asks   *Has this song we want to write*
already been written
We sit cross legged   silent for a long moment
begin to remember
when we were divided by hate   reed   bigotry

Begin to remember when someone bid us imagine
It's easy if you try"
These words become a sound key
to high school gym Hootenanny

boyfriend Fred   long gone to drugs
strums his guitar and wails   *There's no Heaven*

We sit with our wrinkles faces like tattered quilts   high notes long forgotten
agree that revered songs like John's have survived   like family secrets passed down
sonic keepers of a sacred flame

* Inspired by Imagine by John Lennon
Joan Baez, Joannie Michell, Judy Colins

Wandering with Adagio*
By Marianne Lyon

        I begin fervent journey
          barely feel textured trail
    morning eyes behold rainbow bluff
            smell sweet brook
              watery light bids me
                verdant woods

          There he sits
        deep luminous stare
    sings his name softly   Adagio
asks if he can slow-walk with me
        says trail is patient
sonorous   abundant in wonders

          I open to him
      maybe a worthy companion
        to unfold joy and grief
      balanced in my heart when
        our stepping hears
       crescendoing murmur
    arising from threaded path—
     string orchestra humming
          in minor key

We walk as one melodic line   carrying nothing but ourselves   harmonic path accompanies slopes gently a distant tension forbids us reach a resting but gives way to more meandering   Ardent   we keep sustained trekking   will our destination to appear   when Adagio smiles like a phrase marking   bids us stop untie a rare moment of silence

We feel suspended, so light
as if we might lift,
float away like seeds of
a summer dandelion

*Inspired by *Adagio* by Samuel Barber

Squeeze Box*
By Marianne Lyon

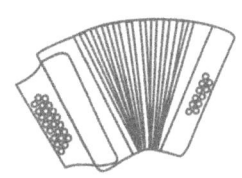

Surges of sound fill lit room
mesmerized with flying fingers
giddy madness overtakes
my bewildered expression

I squeal fortissimo: "How can a box make music?"
He plays you with his whole body   Squeeze Box he calls you
arms surround your cartoon-like figure you perch proud
on his pumping knee he dances the soft bellowing wears a redemptive smile
like he is in church   saying his penance   sins washing away

You and dad   a festive couple
you coax him to sing
words run together
like a creek of laughter
his face changes
when you rest in his arms

All day I inhale you spinning gold in his lap   his nimble fingers
skate your warm ivory ribs   feel liquid palpitations
like harmonic waterfall splashing   from your lungs

He plays you with his whole body
You   a portal of delight
always at his fingertips
when he caresses
you stretch him open
like spring melt-water
guttering down the street

Dedicated to my musical Father

Basso Continuo*
By Marianne Lyon

Remember   beneath Grams lilac bush
only three years old
first soft song was imagined
Your deep contralto voice
heartbeat vibration   beckoned from
across summer lawn

*Understand   always wanted to
muse with you   glide above
unwavering rhythm
copy your repetitive phrase
harmonize us into nimble compositions*

Remember   you were present
accompanying chants of reverence for my dolls
whispering duets with secret friend   Charlie
You   my satellite   encouraged ruckus
wailing of Joni's *Chelsea Morning*
Puccini's *Un mio bambino caro*

*Understand   always wanted to know you
to mimic   parrot   imitate
don't know when it happened
but I began to feel you inside of me*

not across fresh mowed lawn
not in dim cellar with my dolls
not on stage bedecked in operatic gown
Reposed in me this frosty season
you urge us trill a duet with untiring zeal

Understand   my hair partially silvered
High notes   impossible
But your inside-me-voice nudges
I begin to match your contralto timbre
Suddenly   a rendition of first ditty
under Grams lilac bush slowly resurrects
requests a growing old revision

* Inspired by *Pachelbel's Canon: Basso Continuo (repeating bass line)*

Where Love Resides*
By Geoffrey K. Leigh

I thought my love had fled away
Gone with you to forever stay
My loneliness surged both night and day
A sullen and broken heart to enforce

I loved you dear, with all my heart
Even the day when you'd depart
Until I found a new place to start
When I discovered my love's source

As love survived and showed its strength
Even at waters edge, close to the bank
I know in part I have you to thank
For love's valor became my force

Sometimes in life the courage to stand
Is brought about by another's hand
And you find yourself in a foreign land
With only inner love to stay the course

When love blazes with the power to save
It burns all sediment with fiery wave
Until there is only the fire you crave
Leaving nothing in it's path for remorse

Yet love survived and showed me strength
Even at waters edge, when my heart sank
I know in the end its my heart I thank
For love's origin becomes my force

*Inspired by <u>Living Truth</u>, written and performed by Kirtana.

The creative adult is the child who survived.

— **Ursula Le Guin**

A question to consider for your writing:

What might you compose when you hear an echo bid a shadow to waltz?

About the Authors

*Creativity is piercing the mundane
to find the marvelous.*

— Bill Moyers

Geoffrey K. Leigh

I write to create, I create to live, I live to inspire.

I taught, conducted workshops and wrote academic papers for three decades before moving to Napa Valley, land on which I never set foot until searching for my ideal relocation. For the first time in my life, this felt like "Home." This verdant valley embraced my soul upon first exploration, enticing my desire to reside in this place of farming and magical creation. Here vines are nurtured and grape nectar becomes the foundation for crafting, living, laughing, connecting, which, in turn, invigorates my gratitude and creativity. I yearn that something in this work will inspire you to write, to share yourself, your artistry with others. Push away the judgment, the tendency to dismiss and diminish what you do. If you are not happy with the outcome, feel the encouragement to do better. When you read, copy someone else's work until you find your own improved manner of expressing your heart, feelings, in more creative ways than used in the past. Most of all, keep writing. Expression has difficulty improving without practice.

A writer at times would shrink
When people would say his works stink
Then he found his core voice
Providing him with more choice
Now he just gives them a smile and a wink

Marianne C. Lyon

Everyday heroes they were
Did not tell me   only to forget
but involved me   then   I truly learned
they were candles   consuming themselves
to light the way for me

Grew up in a mining town in Montana. I was surrounded by songs in English Croatian Latin. Intrigued by yodeling whistling harmonizing composing on the spot. I was embraced by so many who nudged me sing and create my own songs. For 43 years   I taught music including the International School of Brussels and Hong Kong International. Enjoyed writing poetry and was honored to be published in numerous journals and magazines. A dear candle-friend nudged me to apply for the Poet Laureate of Napa County. I was chosen with the honor from 2021-2023. My hope is that this book will be a candle flame igniting your passion for writing. Nudging you to pick up your pen   waltz to your computer or a morning walk with nature   and allow words   phrases and verses to sprout and bloom. I invite you to be a beacon for yourself and for others.

Anyone can be a candle
we all have gifts to share
All it takes is intention
and the willingness to care

www.ingramcontent.com/pod-product-compliance
Lightning Source LLC
Chambersburg PA
CBHW070539010526
44118CB00012B/1178